The Meaning of Happiness

Alan W. Watts

The Meaning

PERENNIAL LIBRARY
HARPER & ROW, PUBLISHERS
NEW YORK

of Happiness

The Quest for Freedom
of the Spirit in Modern
Psychology and the
Wisdom of the East

First PERENNIAL LIBRARY edition published 1970

CONTENTS

PREFACE TO THE SECOND EDITION

This book first appeared in the Spring of 1940, at the very moment when the Second World War broke loose in all its violence. Despite the fact that it was published at that most inauspicious time and the fact that its title gave it the outward appearance of a type of "inspirational literature" far removed from its inner content, *The Meaning of Happiness* has been "sold out" for many years—during which I have received repeated requests for its republication.

I have hesitated to comply with this demand because in so many ways my ideas have gone far beyond the philosophy of a book written when I was only twenty-four years old. Yet this book and an even earlier book, *The Spirit of Zen*, remain the favorites of many readers. Setting aside, however, certain immaturities of style and organization, as well as of certain lines of development, the essential theme of this book is, for me, as valid and as important as ever. It has continued as the basic insight of all that I have written subsequently—books in which I have tried to express it in terms of a variety of differing philosophical and religious "languages."

This theme is concerned with the realization of "happiness" in the Aristotelian and Thomistic sense of man's true end or destiny, in which sense happiness means union with God, or, in Oriental terms, harmony with the Tao, or moksha, or nirvana. The point on which I have insisted in many different ways is, in brief, that this special and supreme order of happiness is not a result to be attained through action, but a fact to be realized through knowledge. The sphere of action is to express it, not to gain it.

The exposition of this theme involves a number of peculiar logical and psychological difficulties. From a rigorously logical point of view, the words in which this theme is stated mean exactly nothing. In the terms of the great Oriental philosophies, man's un-happiness is rooted in the feeling of anxiety which attends his sense of being an isolated individual or ego, separate from "life" or "reality" as a whole. On the other hand, happiness—a sense of harmony, completion, and wholeness—comes with the realization that the feeling of isolation is an illusion. In fact, that which feels itself to be the separate, individual consciousness is identical with that universal and undivided Reality of which all things are manifestations.

The Meaning of Happiness explains that the psychological equivalent of this doctrine is a state of mind called "total acceptance," a yes-saying to everything that we experience, the unreserved acceptance of what we are, of what we feel and know at this and every moment. To say, as in the Vedanta, that "All is Brahman," is to say that this whole universe is to be accepted. To put it in another way, at each moment we are what we experience, and there is no real possibility of being other than what we are. Wisdom therefore consists in accepting what we are, rather than in struggling fruitlessly to be something else, as if it were possible to run away from one's own feet.

But if you cannot run away from your feet, you cannot run after them either. If it is impossible to escape from reality, from what *is now*, it is equally impossible to accept or embrace it. You cannot kiss your own lips. Speaking logically, the idea of accepting one's experience in its totality means nothing. For "yes" has meaning only in relation to "no," so that if I say "Yes" to *everything* the word ceases to have any content. To abolish all valleys is to get rid of all mountains. By the same logic, it is equally meaningless to say, "All is Brahman," for statements which are applied to all experiences whatsoever add nothing to our knowledge. When I have said that this whole universe is life, reality, Tao, or Brahman, I have said no more than that everything is everything!

It is easy, then, to sympathize with the reviewer of this book who said, "The mountain has labored and brought forth a mouse." Yet he was mistaken in one slight respect. There was no mouse. And in this tremendous trifle lies the real significance of the book—the meaning which was hidden between the lines because it could not be stated in the words. For between the lines is the paper, the seeming emptiness or nothing, on which the words are printed and which is quite essential to their being printed at all. In a rather similar way, Reality or Brahman is the essential basis of every thing and experience. If I say that paper underlies every word on this page, I might perhaps be understood as saying something like this:

Paper	underlies	every	word	on	this	page
Paper	Paper	Paper	Paper	Paper	Paper	Paper

which is neither sensible nor true.

Just as the words cannot "utter" the paper beneath them, because the paper is not another word, so logic cannot express Reality. In logic, words mean nothing if they do not describe particular experiences. But just as the paper is not a word,

Reality or Brahman is not a particular experience. The statement "All is Brahman" is indeed nonsense if "Brahman" is held, like most other words, to denote a special experience. Yet if Brahman is nothing that we can experience, why trouble to talk about it at all? Am I not saying a great many words about something of which I know nothing?

Here is the whole point of the non-existent mouse over which the mountain labored. I do not know Brahman just as I do not see sight. If I *am* Reality, I cannot grasp it. The life, the Tao, which is the experience of this and all moments I can neither escape nor accept. Every attempt to escape from life or to accept life is as much a vicious circle, as plain an absurdity as trying to know knowledge, to feel feeling, or to burn fire.

> It is only when you seek it that you lose it.
> You cannot take hold of it, nor can you get rid of it;
> While you can do neither, it goes on its own way.
> You remain silent and it speaks; you speak and it is silent.

So what?

So that is what millions of human beings make themselves perfectly miserable trying to do. The laboring of the mountain is the fantastic effort of man to grasp the mystery of life, to find God, to attain happiness, to lay hold on absolute, eternal Being. He clutches at his own hand. He seeks what he has never lost. He suffocates from holding his breath.

This absurdity is only possible on the basis of the feeling that "I" am one thing and "life" or "reality" another, that the knower is separate from his knowledge, the known. This book suggests a total acceptance of experience by way of what is called in Buddhism *upaya*—a device for bringing about an awakening. The hope is that in *trying* to accept life totally one will discover, not in theory alone but in fact, that "whosoever would save his life shall lose it," because one is attempting the impossible task of self-love. The psyche of the average man is in a perfect knot of tension through trying to lay a firm, permanent hold on the life which is its own essence. The attempt to "accept" life tightens this knot to the point where the very impossibility of the task reveals its absurdity.

When this is realized in fact, and, I repeat, not in theory alone, there comes into being that state of liberation or release from self-tension which is the meaning of moksha and nirvana, and Tao—the creative power of life—flows forth freely, no longer blocked by the attempt to turn it back on itself.

Written so long after the book itself, this is perhaps more of an epilogue than a preface, and the reader may do well to refer to it again after what follows it in the space of pages but precedes it in the course of time.

ALAN W. WATTS

The American Academy of Asian Studies,
San Francisco, 1952.

Books on happiness are generally speaking of two kinds. There are those which tell us how to become happy by changing our circumstances, and those which tell us how to become happy by changing ourselves. And then, if such books are not mere philosophy, both kinds proceed to give practical advice as to the ways and means in which happiness may be attained, describing a spiritual, psychological or material technique to achieve the desired result.

This book falls into neither of these two categories, its author believing that happiness of the profoundest kind is beyond the reach of any technique under the sun. Although he claims that this book is strictly practical, it does not name a single thing which one can *do* in order to become happy. Naturally it will be asked, "If there is nothing that one can do either to oneself or to one's circumstances in order to become happy, is any purpose to be served in writing a book to state such a dismal conclusion?" But the conclusion is not dismal. To put it bluntly, it is possible in a certain sense to become happy without doing anything about it. We do not go quite so far as to say that, without knowing it, man is already more happy than he has ever dreamed. Obviously, this is not true, although it is very nearly true. For the object of this book is to prove to men and women something about themselves as they are now, which, if understood, at once creates the greatest happiness that man can know. By this is not meant a state of mere emotional and mental comfort or gayety, but rather an inward experience of the spirit which persists through the deepest suffering.

As this book is written primarily for laymen, the author hopes he will be forgiven for calling rather frequently on two departments of knowledge which are usually the special preserve of the learned, namely the philosophy of ancient Asia and certain aspects of modern psychology. He has therefore had to employ a number of special terms because the English language is not always equipped to express certain ideas in plain, straightforward words without lamentable confusion and misunderstanding. He trusts, therefore, that such terms are sufficiently explained, but asks it to be borne in mind that every human being speaks a different language and that sometimes it seems as if words were made to conceal thoughts. Now it is often that the specialist, the professional philosopher or psychologist, delights in the precise use of words, and sometimes he will find this book extremely irritating because it uses words whose meaning is quite clear to the "man-in-the-street" but utterly obscure to the philosopher. For example we may take such words as "life," "nature," "love," "fate," or "soul." These words have been used freely because they are *living* words, which, if read without hypercritical sophistry, can mean more than any number of special terms. Thus it will be seen that the author has tried to steer a middle course between the two obscurities of over-simplicity and over-technicality.

Some orientalists and psychologists may complain that their researches have been grossly misused and misinterpreted in some of the conclusions which have been drawn from them. Various aspects of Christian theology may seem to have suffered in the same way, but, for those who wish to inquire more closely into original sources, notes giving "chapter and verse" have been provided at the end of the book. One thing more must be said for both laymen and specialists, and particularly for reviewers. Each chapter in this book is an introduction to the last, upon the subject of which the whole validity of the central theme depends and apart from which it should not be judged.

In conclusion the author wishes to thank Dr. Charles G. Taylor of New York for his advice on preparing an important section of the manuscript, and also the Rev. Sokei-an Sasaki for allowing the author to consult his translation of an otherwise unavailable text.

ALAN W. WATTS

New York City,
January, 1940.

Sometimes naked, sometimes mad,
Now as a scholar, now as a fool,
Thus they appear on earth—
The free men!

Hindu poem.

INTRODUCTION

During the last fifty years the mental life of Western civilization has been invaded by two forces which are having a profound though gradual influence on our attitude to life. One of these forces has emerged from the West itself, while the other has come from far distant lands. At first sight no one saw that these two influences had anything in common, but with the growth of experience it is becoming clear not only that they are, in spirit, closely bound together, but also that their effects reach far beyond the places where they are professionally studied.

The first, a product of the West, is the form of scientific psychology associated with the names of Freud and Jung, which bases its research and practice on the idea of the unconscious mind and whose object is the purely practical one of healing the mentally sick. The second force is a product of the Orient, and is the wisdom of ancient India and China which has been revealed to us in its fullness only in comparatively recent years by the labors of scholars in Sanskrit, Pali, Chinese, and Japanese. At first it was thought that the wisdom they revealed was of little more than academic interest, and had the *misérable vanité des savants* had its way the treasures of Hindu, Buddhist, and Taoist thought would have remained as much a preserve for the merely erudite as Roman law and Egyptian hieroglyphics. It was soon recognized, however, that this treasure of spiritual literature was not only beautiful to read and consider; it was also seen to be of practical use. The ideas and precepts contained in it were not only as true for our own time and place as for the ancient East; they were also, if not entirely new to us, suggestive of new approaches and new ways of adjustment to problems very close to our hearts, and seemed to offer ways of amplifying the wisdom of the West.

An inquiry into the relations between Oriental religion and the psychology of the unconscious might be of interest to those who specialize in these things, but the object of this book is much wider. For neither was originally evolved for the express benefit of specialists; their purpose was and is to assist mankind as a whole, and because there are many close likenesses in their method of inquiry they have come to similar conclusions—or perhaps it would be better to say "working hypotheses." This form of psychology has taught that man's conscious self and its various faculties of reason and emotion are the outward appearance of a hidden, mental universe in which the true origin of his thoughts and deeds is to be found. In other words, it would say that man's true self goes a long way beyond his conscious "ego" or "I" which is the unknowing instrument of the unconscious, or of "nature-in-man." When the ego is unaware of this condition it arrogates to itself powers and capabilities which set it in conflict with the unconscious, and from this conflict arise the greater part of our psychological troubles. But when we become conscious of the limitations of the ego and understand its relation to the unconscious, then there is some chance of true mental health. This is strikingly similar to many Oriental teachings if we can substitute for the term "unconscious" or "nature-in-man" such Oriental terms as Tao, Brahman and the like, which mean the (to us) unknown self of both man and life, or nature.

It will therefore be necessary to explore these similarities to some extent, but it is even more important to consider what the invasion of our civilization by these two forces can mean for ordinary men and women whose interest in such subjects is purely practical. For the number of people who have such an interest in either or both of these things is much greater than is generally realized. Moreover many religious cults of the present day are considerably influenced by Oriental ideas, especially the many forms of theosophy, occultism and mysticism patronized by so many people whom the ordinary churches fail to satisfy. Therefore we have to ask just what contribution these two forces have to make to the happiness of the average human being who wishes to benefit from them without becoming a psychological or Oriental specialist.

Many people have tried to answer this question from the standpoint of psychology alone or Oriental philosophy alone. But few attempts have been made to explore the possibilities from the standpoint of both. Why should this be done? Because there are certain elements in Oriental philosophy which are utterly unsuited to Western life and these elements are not easily seen unless brought to the attention by a critical method which only this psychology of the unconscious can provide. Furthermore, psychology has much to gain from the ancient East. In the West psychology is a new science; in the East it is very ancient, and in fact it is not correct to speak of Oriental *philosophy* at all, for in no sense is it philosophy as we understand it. Essentially it is neither speculative nor academic; it is experimental and practical, and is much closer to psychology than philosophy.

But the need for a rapprochement between the two has for some time been recognized by the foremost living practitioner of this particular type of psychology—C. G. Jung of Zürich.[1]

My experience in my practice (he writes) has been such as to reveal to me a quite new and unexpected approach to eastern wisdom. But it must be well understood that I did not have as a starting point a more or less adequate knowledge of Chinese philosophy. On the contrary, when I began my life-work in the practice of psychiatry and psychotherapy, I was completely ignorant of Chinese philosophy, and it is only later that my professional experiences have shown me that in my technique I had been unconsciously led along that secret way which for centuries has been the preoccupation of the best minds of the East.

Because of this admission many of his contemporaries have charged Jung with mysticism and departure from strict scientific method. Such charges, however, are based on a very understandable ignorance of the true character of Oriental psychology and of those aspects of it with which Jung has been concerned. These aspects have little or no connection with metaphysical speculation and religious doctrine as such; nor have they a connection with certain sensational forms of occultism so attractive to those who lack discrimination.

Our problem is therefore this: What do Eastern and Western psychology taken together have to say about the elusive and pressing subject of human happiness? For this subject is especially the province of psychology as distinct from what we usually understand as religion, or even philosophy. Often the purpose of religion is supernatural experience and philosophy is primarily interested in Truth, and their concern with happiness, in its profoundest sense, is indirect. This indeed is yet another reason why Oriental wisdom and the psychology of the unconscious have to be taken together. It is the only profitable way of considering the collective possibilities of psychology from the East and from the West. As we have seen, Oriental wisdom is psychology rather than philosophy and theology, and the schools of Freud and Jung are the only practical forms of Western psychology which have any relation to it. Unlike the older schools of psychology their object is not simply to observe, tabulate and comment on the mental behavior of man. On the contrary, their method is empirical and its aim is to heal and give happiness of the deepest and most abiding kind. This too may be said of Oriental psychology, for the experience or state of mind at which it aims is a conscious harmony with life and nature both in external circumstances and in oneself.

The discovery of this kind of happiness is perhaps the chief desire of man, though it is not always expressed quite in that way, for to many the word "happiness" has unfortunate associations. But I use it here because it is the only ordinary, everyday word we have to denote an oddly elusive and mysterious type of experience, the kind of experience that runs away from you the moment you begin to look for it. That highly intensified form of happiness which is spiritual experience behaves in just the same way; it is like trying to catch soap with wet fingers. Oriental psychology is particularly well experienced in this elusive art—need one call to mind the popular Chinese proverb, "Softly, softly, catchee monkey"?—and it seems necessary that in considering a problem which occupies so many of our thoughts we should call upon the psychology of East and West alike.

The elusiveness of all kinds of happiness is common knowledge, for have we not the saying, "Those who search for happiness never find it"? This is especially true of that complete kind of happiness which does not depend on external events, which belongs to the very nature of the individual and remains unaffected by suffering. It persists through both joy and sorrow, being a spiritual undertone which results from the positive and whole-hearted acceptance of life in all its aspects. This acceptance, known under many names in the psychology of religion, comes to pass when the individual, the ego, surrenders the conceit of personal freedom and power, realizing that it depends absolutely on that inner, unknown universe which is nature in the human soul. It only exists as an ego to fulfill the purpose of that universe—a purpose which, in one sense, it cannot help serving, but which, in another sense, it does not appreciate when laboring under the conceit of personal freedom and self-sufficiency. When, however, that conceit is abandoned an altogether new and more powerful freedom is known—the freedom of union or harmony between man and life.[2] But freedom, union, harmony, life—these are vague terms, and the things they signify seem to be as elusive as the terms are vague. To them also applies the old truism that those who search for them do not find them. Such ideas are the commonplaces of popular philosophy and psychology, but in this instance the commonplace is but the familiar entrance to a largely unknown and labyrinthine territory of the spirit. Less than a hair's-breadth divides the self-evident from the subtle, and the danger is that in ignoring something that lies right at our feet we may trip over it through overmuch concentration upon remote parts of the horizon or the heavens.

The very saying, "Those who search for happiness never find it," raises a host of complications for it will be asked, "If happiness is not found by searching, how is it found?" to which might be added, "If happiness is found by not-searching, or by searching for something else, is not this merely an indirect way of searching for happiness, as it were by a trick or deceit? Surely the important thing is not the means employed, direct or indirect, but the motive for employing them." There is still another preliminary question that might be asked on this point: "Would it not be true to say that one who does not search for happiness, either directly or indirectly, already has it? Therefore does not the saying that those who search for it do not find it amount to this: those who have it do not search for it; those who do not have it search for it, and thus cannot find it?" In other words, happiness is something which you either have or haven't, and if you haven't there is nothing you can do about it except wait for the Grace of God which is something quite outside your control.

Whatever the precise answers to these questions it is generally agreed that happiness cannot be had by any form of direct striving. Like your shadow, the more you chase it, the more it runs away. It is not surprising therefore that in both ancient religions and modern psychology man is advised to relax his self-assertive efforts and acquire a certain passivity of soul, encouraging thereby a state of receptivity or acceptance, which Christianity would describe as easing-up the tumult of self-will in order that it may give place to the will of God. It is as if man were to empty his soul in order that the gifts of the spirit might pour in, on the principle that nature abhors a vacuum. But whether it is called the giving-up of self, submitting to the will of God, accepting life, releasing the tension of striving for happiness or letting oneself go with the stream of life, the essential principle is one of relaxation.

"Relaxation" is a word often heard nowadays—advertisers, teachers of dancing, music, swimming, physical culture, riding, drama, and business efficiency, doctors, psychologists and preachers, all use it in their varying subjects, its popularity being increased by the nervous tension of modern life. It may be used to mean anything from reading a mystery story or the secret of a ballerina's art to the way of life of a sage whose soul is in perfect harmony with the universe. For, like "happiness," it is a word of many meanings and is used quite as casually, and this is not the only similarity between the two. Relaxation is something just as elusive as happiness; it is something which no amount of self-assertive striving can obtain, for as it is in a certain sense the absence of effort, any effort to achieve it is self-defeating.

These two words have many other equivalents, some of them much more high-sounding, and in writing and conversation men have exalted them to the skies and dragged them in the mud. There need, however, be no apology for using them, for they belong to common, everyday speech and even if countless associations make their meaning confused, confusion is worse confounded by introducing a new, exotic jargon when familiar and accepted words already exist. Even if they call too strongly to mind trite little mottoes on greeting cards or advertisements for someone's cigarettes or patent medicine, such associations can be overshadowed by the knowledge that these same things, under perhaps different names, have been the chief preoccupation of the greatest minds on earth. Other words have had a like fortune, notably the word "love" which men have made to mean everything from brute lust to God Himself. Such words may drop loosely from our tongues as if the things which they signify were as common as hats and houses; in a few senses they are, but in others they are things which, however common in our dreams, are little known and seldom found in reality. Often they seem quite close to us, as if we should come upon them round the next bend of the road, but this is their special peculiarity. In this they are like a carrot dangled before a donkey's nose from a stick attached to his collar; if he chases it, it runs ahead of him; if he stands still, it remains where it is, so near and yet so far.

The fact that happiness is associated with relaxation does not mean that it is impossible to be happy in the midst of strenuous effort, for to be truly effective great effort must, as it were, revolve upon a steady, unmoving center. The problem before us is how to find such a center of relaxed balance and poise in man's individual life—a center whose happiness is unshaken by the whirl that goes on around it, which creates happiness because of itself and not because of external events, and this in spite of the fact that it may experience those events in all their aspects and extremes from the highest bliss to the deepest agony.

If, therefore, as both Oriental and Western psychology suggest, the most profound happiness is to be found in a conscious union or harmony between the individual and the unknown Self, the unconscious, inner universe, it is clear that the problem has a number of peculiar difficulties. These arise for two principal reasons: first, that twentieth-century, civilized man is so centered in his own limited self-consciousness that he is quite unaware of its origin, of the directing forces that lie beneath it; and second, that the real problem is not to bring about a state of affairs which does not as yet exist, but to realize something which is already happening—"as it was in the beginning, is now and ever shall be." For although civilized man *appears* to live only from his self-conscious center, although he *appears* divorced from nature, from a spiritual point of view this is a mere conceit. In other words, at this very moment we have that union and harmony in spite of ourselves; we create spiritual problems simply through not being aware of it, and that lack of understanding causes and in turn is caused by the delusion of self-sufficiency. As Christianity would say, the Grace of God is always being freely offered; the problem is to get man to accept it and give up the conceit that he can save himself by the power of his ego, which is like trying to pick himself up by his own belt. This appears to be a vicious circle, the more so for people who cannot believe in the Christian God, having been deprived of their belief by science and rationality which are essentially powers of self-consciousness. Both Oriental and Western psychology, however, state the problem in a rather different way. They say that if the ego can be made to look into itself, it will see that its own true nature is deeper than itself, that it derives its faculties and its consciousness from a source beyond individual personality. In other words, the ego is not really a self at all; it is simply a *function* of that inner universe. In much the same way, speech is a function of the human being, and it is possible that one given only the sense of hearing might think that the voice is the man. But in order to fulfill its function the ego must be self-conscious—a faculty at once valuable and dangerous, for if the ego is deceived by that faculty it falls into the vicious circle of trying to find happiness by its own power.

Vicious circles create ever-increasing complications when we attempt to unravel them in their own terms. Therefore in these days people are blinded to the spiritual problem by seeking its answer in the very complex, and even the psychology of the unconscious has not fully delivered itself from the thraldom of complications. But the breaking of the circle is simple if only we can adapt our minds to real simplicity, as distinct from triteness; for this the ego must yield its pride and be humble enough to see something lowly, something which the psychology of Asia has been teaching men to see for thousands of years.

In an altogether odd and apparently mysterious way the whole question of happiness in this sense is far from straightforward. It is unusually complicated because in fact it is unusually simple; its solution lies so close to us and is so self-evident that we have the greatest difficulty in seeing it, and we must complicate it in order to bring it into focus and be able to discuss it at all. This may seem a terrible paradox, but it is said that a paradox is only a truth standing on its head to attract attention. For there are certain truths which have to be stood on their heads before they can be noticed at all; in the ordinary way they are so simple that we fail to perceive them. Our own faces are an example of this. Nothing could be more obvious and self-evident than a man's own face; but oddly enough he cannot see it at all unless he introduces the complication of a mirror, which shows it to him reversed. The image he sees is his face and yet is not his face, and this is a form of paradox. And here is the reason for all our vagueness and uncertainty concerning the things of the spirit, for if our eyes cannot see themselves, how much less can that something which looks through the eyes see itself.

Therefore we have to find some way of overcoming the

difficulty, some way of understanding the most obvious thing in the world, a thing which is ordinarily overlooked because our thoughts and feelings are moving in much more complicated channels. To see it they have to be brought down to a level of humility, not fearful and kowtowing, but having the most direct and childlike openness of mind—"for He hath put down the mighty from their seat, and hath exalted the humble and meek." It is not surprising, therefore, that these deepest truths of the spirit are often missed by people of the most brilliant and penetrating intellect. This is not to say, however, that they will be any more readily understood by mere lack of intellect. Such insight comes neither with brilliance nor dullness of the mind, for the one is deluded with its own proud glittering and the other just fails to register. To understand such tremendous simplicity one has just to open the eyes of the mind and see; there is no secret about it, for it stands before us in open daylight, as large as life. In the words of the Chinese sage Tao-wu, "If you want to see, see directly into it; but when you try to think about it, it is altogether missed."

Therefore when it is said that those who search for happiness never find it perhaps the truth is that there is no need to search for it. Like our own eyes, it may be going along with us all the time; only when we turn round to try to see it we make fools of ourselves. Thus a Chinese poem says:[3]

It is so clear that it takes long to see.
You must know that the fire which you are seeking
Is the fire in your own lantern,
And that your rice has been cooked from the very beginning.

The Meaning of Happiness

Almost everyone knows the story of the goose that laid the golden eggs. A man and his wife had a mysterious goose that from time to time favored them by laying a golden egg. When this had been going on for some weeks they began to think it rather tiresome of the goose to part with its gold so gradually, for they imagined that it carried a store of such eggs inside itself. Not having the sense to weigh the creature first and find out if it was much heavier than a goose should be, they decided to kill it and cut it open. As might be expected, they found only one ordinary, dead goose, void of gold eggs and unable to produce any more.

There were once scientists, too, who were similarly disappointed when they searched the human anatomy to find an organ that might be described as the soul; there are still scholars who analyze Beethoven down to the last semiquaver and Shakespeare to the last pronoun to find the secret of their genius, and there are also theologians who do much the same thing with the words of the Bible to discover the nature of God. And it is yet the hope of even the most advanced science that the universe will yield up its mysteries, its last mighty secret, to those who dissect its tiniest fragments, learning more and more about less and less. This is known as not being able to see the wood for the trees. It is by no means an error peculiar to scientists and scholars, for the fable of the golden eggs is an ancient tale of human nature.

We have a saying about the virtue of being able to "see life whole," for all meaning is in wholeness. There could be no golden eggs without the goose, and however tiresome, slow, and stupid the goose might be, he resembled life in that he was an interplay of opposites: he was slow, but his eggs were gold, and if you cut him to pieces to gather the gold and discard the slowness you were left with nothing but a corpse. This will also happen if you carve up the human body to find the mysterious source of its vitality or if you separate the flower of a plant from its muddy roots. Something very similar happens in a much more important way when men love life and hate death or cling to youth and reject old age, which is like expecting a mountain to have only one slope— that which goes up, whereas to be a mountain it must go up and down. For the meaning is in the whole, and not only the meaning but the very existence of the thing. Indeed, we are only aware of life and life is only able to manifest itself because it is divided into innumerable pairs of opposites: we know motion by contrast with stillness, long by short, light by darkness, heat by cold, and joy by sorrow.

Therefore to see life whole is to understand these opposing qualities as essential to its existence, without trying to interfere, without dissecting the body of the universe so that its pleasant portions may be preserved and its unpleasant cast away. This is what the philosophic Hindu understands when, looking at the most terrible things, he can say, "*Sarvam kalvidam Brahman*"—"This, too, is Brahman," that divine Being of whose Self[1] each single thing is a changing aspect. And to him this Brahman is not merely the whole universe any more than seeing life whole is seeing the whole of life; in this sense Brahman is rather the wholeness, even the holiness, of life which can be destroyed only in the fantasy world of our own minds. Therefore those who attempt to destroy it carry, as it were, corpses in their thoughts which corrupt and poison their souls. In the life to which they cling in horror of death, the pleasure in fear of pain, the wealth in fear of poverty, and the youth in fear of age, they hold only to the world's dismembered limbs. Yet though they may not know it the dismembering and the consequent suffering exist only in themselves; they *think* they can take the whole apart, but it is a poor illusion. Its only result is that for all their clinging their life, pleasure, wealth, and youth have the taint of unhappiness because, having cut them off to possess them forever, they are no more alive. Thus it is not surprising that some few "wise ones" having come to grief in this way cry out that pleasure and wealth are sins wherein no happiness is to be found. But fire is not evil because it burns your fingers if you try to catch hold of it; it is only dangerous.

THE PROBLEM OF OPPOSITES

We call such things as life and death "opposites," but this is not altogether a satisfactory name seeing that it implies a state of opposition and hence of conflict. But life and death are in conflict only in the mind which creates a war between them out of its own desires and fears. In fact life and death are not opposed but complementary, being the two essential factors of a greater life that is made up of living and dying just as melody is produced by the sounding and silencing of individual notes. Life feeds on death, and its very movement is only possible and apparent because of the continuous birth and death of cells, the absorption of nourishment and the discarding of waste, which in its turn provides a fertile soil from which new life can spring. For vitality is a cycle whose completion requires both upward movement and downward movement just as light cannot manifest itself without the whole motion of the light-wave from start to finish; if these waves could be divided into half or quarter waves the light would disappear. So also in the biological realm we have two opposite yet complementary sexes, male and female; beings are divided in this way in order to reproduce themselves, and the meaning of man and woman is the child without which there would be no point in having two sexes at all. Thus they are the two legs upon which our life stands, and when one is cut away the whole collapses.

These so-called opposites present man with a difficult problem, for there is a longing in his heart for eternity and victory over death, a longing which is misdirected because in life as he knows it he himself is one of those opposites and thus is apparently set against something over which he can never triumph. For the foundation of our life as we know it is the opposition between ourselves and the universe, between that which is "I" and that which is not "I." Here again are two things which are complementary rather than opposed, for it is obvious that the self cannot exist without the universe and that the universe cannot exist without the multitude of selves and entities of which it is composed. But from the point of view of suffering, struggling man this fact, however obvious, is purely abstract. Moreover, the existence of the universe depends apparently only on the impersonal multitude of selves of which there is an inexhaustible supply; it does not depend on any particular self. Indeed, nature seems astonishingly callous and wasteful in its treatment of individual selves, and it is therefore not surprising that man should rebel when treated with the same callous disregard for individuality as is the insect. It even seems that here there is an actual conflict which does not exist solely in the mind, for with one hand nature lavishes the most amazing skill on the creation of individuals and even on their preservation, while with the other it treats them as if they were no more than the dust from which they rose. But if one or the other of nature's hands were tied the world would either choke itself from overabundance of life or be altogether depopulated. Nevertheless, from the individual point of view the process is wasteful and callous. Man might assist nature to a greater economy by regulating the reproduction of his own kind and by adapting himself to nature instead of trying to fight it. But this requires a concerted social effort that might take thousands of years to accomplish, and hence is of little consequence to individuals living in the turmoil of the twentieth century.

However, scientific measures for the removal of suffering are here beside the point, for it is doubtful whether the resulting increase of comfort would be welcomed if it were sufficient to upset the balance of the opposites. Just as too much light blinds the eyes, too much pleasure numbs the senses; to be apparent it needs contrast. But the problem of man's conflict with the universe remains. We can present any number of straightforward, rational solutions, justifying the existence of these uncomfortable opposites and the unfortunate but necessary operations of natural law. It is the easiest thing in the world to philosophize, telling man how glad he should be that he suffers, seeing that otherwise he would be unable to feel joy. But when it comes to the point such talk is found to be remote and abstract, leaving the heart unconvinced even if the head is satisfied.

For here we are touching the very root of man's unhappiness, and to these regions the sweetly reasonable voice of pure philosophy does not penetrate. Whatever may be said about the need for basing one's attitude to life on a universal as distinct from a personal point of view, the difficulty is that in the ordinary way man does not feel universal. His center is himself and his consciousness peeps out through windows in a wall of flesh; he does not feel his consciousness as existing in things outside of himself, seeing through others' eyes or moving with others' limbs. And the world outside that wall is threatening, so much so that he does everything possible to fortify himself against it, surrounding himself with a barricade of possessions and illusions to hide himself from the world and the world from him. Within this fortress he strives to guard and preserve the thing he calls his life, but he might as well try to imprison sunlight in a room by pulling down the blind or trap wind by shutting the door. To enjoy wind you must let it blow past you and feel it against bare flesh; the same is true of time, for the moment has always gone before it can be seized, and the same is true of life which not even this wall of flesh can hold forever. To feel and understand it you must let it blow past you like the wind as it moves across the earth from void to void. But this is intolerable. It means tearing down the barricade, giving up every security, opening windows both sides of the room so that the draught sweeps through, knocks down the vases, scatters our papers, and upsets the furniture. This is too great a price to pay for having the dust and cobwebs blown out of our souls. Besides, we shall catch cold and sit shivering and sneezing till we go crazy.

> From thy nest every rafter
> > Will rot, and thine eagle-home
> Leave thee naked to laughter
> > Till leaves fall and cold winds come,

So we keep the windows closed and shuttered until we die from suffocation, overwhelmed by stagnant air.

THE FEAR OF FEAR

This is a malady as old as life, born of what Keyserling[2] calls "Original Fear" whose outward aspect psychologists term the "pleasure-pain principle." For as the snail and the tortoise withdraw into their shells, man retires into his castle of illusion. But it is curious that whereas the snail and the tortoise often come out of their shells, man hardly ever comes out of his castle, because he seems to have a much more acute sense of his personal identity, of his distinction from the rest of the universe. The greater the sense of distinction, the greater the tension between the two and the more the pairs of opposites war together in the soul. This tension we call unhappiness, but it is not suggested that it will be overcome by the abolition of "Original Fear," which is in itself a most valuable instinct. If we liked pain as much as pleasure we might shortly become extinct, for it is only this original fear of pain which urges us to self-preservation. Here again we have a pair of opposites, love and fear or like and dislike, mutually essential components of the faculty of feeling, for who does not fear neither loves nor feels. But note the term *original* fear. Man's difficulty is that his fear is seldom original; it is once or many times

7

removed from originality, being not just simple fear but the fear of being afraid.

There are two kinds of tension, creative and destructive, the first as when a string is tensed to produce music and the second as when it is tensed to be broken. Between the opposites there must also be tension if they are to produce life. Of their nature they must move in opposite directions, and yet they must be held together by a relationship and a meaning. By centrifugal force the earth speeds away from the sun; by gravity it is drawn toward it, and hence it moves around it in a circle and is neither frozen nor burned. Thus the movement of the opposites away from each other is original fear, while the tie that binds them is original love. The result is creative tension. But man is not just afraid; he fears the tension caused by his original fear so that his fear is increased. The tension is also increased, growing all the more frightening until it becomes destructive instead of creative. The tie is stretched to breaking point, whereat the opposites tend to shoot apart into utter isolation. Thus when the tension of original fear is accepted man can swing happily upon his orbit; but should he try to escape from that fear he simply adds one fear to another and one tension to another, which is a process that may go on forever. Like a fly caught in a spider's web, the more he struggles, the more he becomes involved.

In this way the tension of the opposites is turned by man into destructive conflict. Clinging to one and fleeing from the other he simply incites the one he flees to assert itself the more. To hate death and change is trying to make life deathless and changeless, and this is a rigid, moribund, living death. Hence the saying, "Cowards die a thousand deaths, but the valiant die but once." For in holding to pleasure in fear of pain man starts the tension, but the real trouble begins when he tries to get rid not only of the pain but of the tension as well, giving himself two enemies instead of one. That pain should arouse fear is as natural as that fire should arouse warmth. But let it stay there, for if we run from our fear it becomes panic, and this is the entrance to a bottomless abyss of self-deception and misery. Man does not like to admit to himself that he is afraid, for this weakens his self-esteem and shakes his faith in the security of his ego. To accept fear would be like accepting death, so he runs from it, and this is the great unhappiness. Sometimes it is expressed in sheer unbridled terror, but more often it is a half-concealed, gnawing anxiety moving in vicious circles to an ever greater intensity. It would have been better to say in the first place, "I am afraid, but not ashamed."

Therefore in struggling with the opposites man perpetually deceives himself. The prizes he tries to pluck away from life and keep solely for his personal use turn moldy because he has severed them from their roots, and nothing that is isolated can live, since the two most important characteristics of life are circulation and change. On the other hand, the troubles which he tries to avoid are the only things which make him aware of his blessings, and if he would love the latter he must fear the former. But he is afraid of fear. These two things make him respectively frustrated and worried, driving him more and more into an attitude of isolation, of separateness from and hostility toward the rest of life, standing huddled and miserable between the devil of circumstances and the deep sea of his own unpredictable and unruly emotions. And in this isolation his spirit perishes.

MAN AND NATURE

Man is as much attached to nature as a tree, and though he walks freely on two legs and is not rooted in the soil, he is by no means a self-sufficient, self-moving, and self-directing entity. For his life he depends absolutely on the same factors as the tree, the worm, and the fly, on the universal powers of nature, life, God, or whatever it may be. From some mysterious source life flows through him unceasingly; it does not just go in at birth and come out at death—he is the channel for an ever moving stream, a stream that carries the blood through his veins, that moves his lungs and brings him air to breathe, that raises his food from the earth and bears the light of the sun to his face. If we look into a single cell of his body we find the universe, for sun, moon, and stars are ceaselessly maintaining it; we find it again if we plumb into the depths of his mind, for there are all the archaic urges of primeval life, both human and animal, and could we look deeper we might find kinship with the plants and rocks. For man is a meeting-place for the interplay of forces from all quarters of the universe, swept through him in a stream which is the power behind all his thoughts and actions, which is indeed more truly man's self than his body or mind, its instruments. This was known to almost all the ancient peoples of the world whose sages taught that all the actions of man were as much expressions of nature's unceasing movement as the sun and the wind—a fact that would be obvious to anyone not born and bred in a place where there was little more to see than human handiwork.

The isolation of the human soul from nature is, generally speaking, a phenomenon of civilization. This isolation *is* more apparent than real, because the more nature is held back by brick, concrete, and machines, the more it reasserts itself in the human mind, usually as an unwanted, violent, and troublesome visitor. But actually the creations of man, his art, his literature, his buildings, differ only in quality, not in kind, from such creations of nature as birds' nests and honeycombs. Man's creations are infinitely more numerous and ingenious, but this very ingenuity, together with his fear, aggravates his feeling of isolation, persuading him that he is a creator in his own right, separate from nature. For once again it would go against his self-esteem to have to admit that his superb faculty of reason and all its works do not make him the master of nature rather than its servant. Bewitched by his power of reason and urged on through fright of his fear man seeks his freedom in isolation from and not union with nature—"whose service is perfect freedom."

Man's struggle for mastery is magnificent and tragic; but it does not work. And the difficulty is not so much in what he does as in what he thinks. If he were to seek union instead of isolation this would not involve what is generally called "getting back to nature"; he would not have to give up his machines and cities and retire to the forests and live in wigwams. He would only have to change his attitude, for the penalties he pays for his isolation are only indirectly on the physical plane. They originate from and are most severe in his mind.

What are these penalties? We give them the broad name of unhappiness, and though this is not something peculiar to civilization, civilization offers us an extreme case especially in the world of to-day. Of course, it is not possible for us to know whether we are any less happy than savages, nor whether we suffer less. All men suffer, now as well as in ancient times, but not all are unhappy, for unhappiness is a reaction to suffering, not suffering itself. Therefore, generally speaking, the primitive was unhappy from his conflict with the *external* forces of nature. But the unhappiness of civilized man is chiefly the result of conflict with natural forces *inside* himself and inside human society, forces that are all the more dangerous and violent because they come in unrecognized and unwanted at the back door.

THE IMPORTANCE OF CONFLICT

The meaning of civilization is nowhere better explained than in the parable of the Prodigal Son.[3]

A certain man had two sons. And the younger of them said to his father, Father, give me the portion of goods that falleth to me. And he divided unto them his living. . . . The younger son gathered all together, and took his journey into a far country, and there wasted his substance in riotous living. And when he had spent all there arose a mighty famine in that land; and he began to be in want. . . . And he would fain have filled his belly with the husks that the swine did eat: and no man gave unto him. And when he came to himself he said, . . . I will arise and go to my father, and will say unto him, Father, I have sinned against heaven and before thee, and am no more worthy to be called thy son: make me as one of thy hired servants. And he arose and came to his father. . . . And the son said unto him, Father, I have sinned against heaven, and in thy sight, and am no more worthy to be called thy son. But the father said to his servants, Bring forth the best robe, and put it on him; and put a ring on his hand, and shoes on his feet: and bring hither the fatted calf, and kill it; and let us eat and be merry. . . . Now his elder son was in the field: and as he came and drew nigh to the house, he heard music and dancing. And he called one of the servants and asked what these things meant. . . . And he was angry, and would not go in: therefore came his father out, and intreated him. And he answering said to his father, Lo, these many years do I serve thee . . . and yet thou never gavest me a kid, that I might make merry with my friends: but as soon as this thy son was come, which hath devoured thy living with harlots, thou hast killed for him the fatted calf. And he said unto him, Son, thou art ever with me, and all that I have is thine. It was meet that we should make merry . . . for this thy brother was dead, and is alive again; and was lost, and is found.

Civilized man is the prodigal, and the primitive is the elder son who always stayed at home—unconsciously in harmony with nature, living more by instinct than intellect and without the civilized man's acute self-consciousness. The primitive differs from us in somewhat the same way as the child differs from the adult. The child has no psychological problems of its own, and even if it has they are only latent and do not manifest themselves until later life. Its inner affairs are managed partly by nature and partly by its parents; not until the sense of self-consciousness is fully developed does it feel that sense of responsibility which arises when we become aware of our power to direct and control our own affairs. But when man attains that state of self-consciousness he becomes a Prodigal; he feels isolated and lonely, and more particularly in his "low" moments is certain that the universe is against him. Superficially his whole culture is a violation of nature; he becomes utterly dependent on his machines and perishes when left to fend for himself against the elements. But soon comes the "famine." In our own day war and economic disorganization are the "famine"; there is no actual scarcity of wealth; men starve only because of human stupidity. In time there are some who "come to themselves," realizing that in some way or other we must return to nature and experience in full consciousness the harmony which the primitive has by unconscious instinct.

But it is not often realized that the apparent departure from nature which we have in civilization is an absolutely essential stage in man's development. Without it we should remain like the elder son in the parable, jealous and unappreciative. For only those who have sinned can understand and appreciate the bliss of redemption. Perhaps, therefore, this wandering away from nature is not so unnatural after all, for it seems that our task is not to go back to nature but forward. The Hindus represent the evolution of man as a circle. Starting at the top he *falls*, instinctively and unconsciously, to the bottom, at which point they say he enters the extreme of materiality and self-consciousness, the age of Kali Yuga. From thereon he must *climb* up the second half of the circle and so return in full consciousness to the point from which he began. But truly to be united with nature again, he must first experience that absolute division between himself and the universe (or life).

At this point, however, two things must be remembered: first, that civilized man's division from nature is only apparent, and it would seem that this very appearance is part of a natural scheme of evolution, something into which we have grown by instinct as the caterpillar grows into a chrysalis; second, that although the return journey is done *in* consciousness, it is not done *by* consciousness, by the efforts of the self-conscious ego. This part of the journey is again as natural of the development of chrysalis into butterfly, and any attempt to force this growth egotistically is like trying to open the chrysalis with tweezers. It only results in keeping us back in the state of acute opposition between ourselves and life.

Here again we meet with the familiar proverb that those who search for happiness do not find it, because they are trying to manufacture it by the very means which defeat it. Therefore the first step on the homeward journey is to understand that we have never actually been cut off from nature at all, that our present acute conflict with life is necessary, is part of a natural purpose and that self-consciousness is not a denial but a fulfillment of natural law. In other words, we have to accept that conflict, because the ego can no more extract itself from it than a tooth can pull itself out of your jaw. The second step arises naturally from the first: by accepting the conflict between itself and life as part of the nature of life, the ego begins to feel itself in harmony with the "dark" side of nature. For the conflict becomes unhappiness only through our desire to escape from it, which adds one tension to another. But when it is accepted we make a paradoxical discovery, namely that by accepting the ego and the conflict which it involves we also accept and become united with that which stands behind the ego and takes on self-conscious form, that is, with nature. (*See diagram.*)

The Historical Background

It is important to consider this problem in relation to its historical background and to discover some of the ways in which the modern divorcement from nature developed. What is said here is true, in the main, only for Western peoples rooted in the European and Christian tradition, which is to say, for the white races. The Oriental has a different problem, at least in its preliminary stages. Of course, it is impossible to say just exactly when the modern conflict began, but an obvious and convenient starting point may

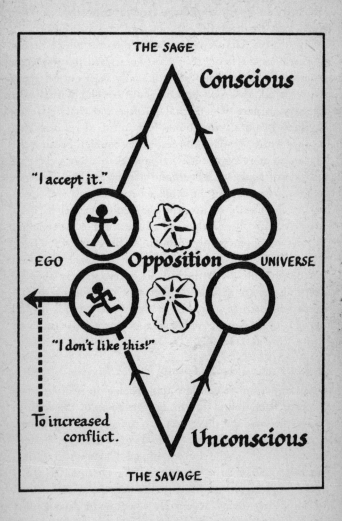

be found in Catholic philosophy of the Middle Ages, although its seeds may be noticed even earlier in late Roman times. Christianity differs from many other religions in according the existence of an immortal soul only to man. The rest of creation exists principally for man's convenience, for no other living creature is of any special significance in the divine plan. This view was never shared by the Hindus or the Chinese, and a Buddhist scripture says that in time even trees and grass shall become Buddhas. But in early Christian thought and practice there was, with few exceptions, an utter lack of concern for anything beyond the salvation of man. It was not surprising, therefore, that Christianity took on an increasingly human or anthropomorphic conception of God. His nature was made to correspond more and more with human reason while the "merely animal," the "irrational" in nature, was more and more identified with the Devil, so that Christianity saw in the beauties of nature little more than a snare for the unwary soul, an essentially sinful world, doomed in the end to perish and give way to a supernatural Paradise.

But the thinkers of the Renaissance did not seem to share this idea, for apparently they were concerned far more with the human and natural than with the spiritual and supernatural. They were the forerunners of the natural sciences. Among them were such men as Leonardo da Vinci and Sir Francis Bacon, men who, as the latter boasted, "took all knowledge for their province." But their preoccupation was still with man, and with the rational aspect of man as distinct from the divine on the one hand, and the bestial on the other. Certainly they found a new interest in the world of animals, trees, flowers, rocks, stars, and mountains, but only to discover therein analogies of the human being; they knew almost nothing of the Chinese and Japanese feeling for nature *as* nature. In their belief "the proper study of mankind was man." and in this, for instance, we find the principal difference between Dante and Shakespeare, the former concerned with man in the supernatural world, the latter with man in his own human world, for "what a peece of worke is man, how noble in reason, how infinit in faculties, in form and moving, how expresse and admirable in action, how like an Angell in apprehension, how like a God!"

The faith of Humanism in the capacity of human reason to solve all problems and subdue all nature made possible the astounding advance of rational science in our epoch, for mathematics and machinery are constructed in the very image of human intellect, sharing its rigid and inevitable logic. But by making a god of this faculty man tends to become machine-like, for reason is essentially the mechanical aspect of the mind. Its laws of logic are as predetermined as the motions of a steam-engine, for a given cause can have only one effect and in this principle the universe is reduced to a machine whose every event has been fated from all eternity. Having discovered the potentialities of his reason man became obsessed with it, and the mechanical Weltanschauung of nineteenth-century science, the Utopia of machines conceived by Wells, and the social ant-hill of Marx were logical results.

Similar changes came to pass in religion. It is particularly significant that the rediscovery of reason should have been accompanied by the birth of Puritan morality and Calvinistic Protestantism with its doctrine of determinism as reactions against "Popish superstition." With the confessional gone and the dark side of life rigidly suppressed man's unmoral nature was denied and rejected by religion as forcibly as his irrational nature was thrown down by science. This is not to say, however, that Protestantism was essentially a rational system; it was not, and consequently came increasingly into conflict with science as the years went by. But the conflict was concerned rather with matters of theory than with those of practice, for though Protestantism was not *doctrinally* rational in the strictest sense of the word, it was rational in its psychology. Its beliefs were based to a great extent upon literal interpretation of the Bible, but its morality was founded mainly on the spirit of Jewish law as set forward in the Old Testament, and it is curious that though doctrinally both Lutheranism and Methodism are anything but legalistic, their standards of morality follow the rigid Puritan tradition. A similar inconsistency may be noted in Calvinism, for belief in predestination, in the doctrine that each man is irrevocably damned or saved from the beginning of the world, might easily encourage moral laxity, seeing that nothing that man can do can affect his ultimate fate. But the result was the very opposite, and nowhere were there more uncompromising moralists than the Calvinists.

Such morality is rational in that it is an attempt to force mankind to conform in thought and action to a rigid and *idealistic* law. This may be giving a rather wide meaning to the term "rational," but in essentials there is little difference between attempts to force man to be moral and attempts to make him reasonable. There may be differences between the moral ideal and the rational ideal, but as they were conceived in the Puritan and Humanist traditions they were ideals contrary to nature in that they ignored that aspect of man's being which corresponds to "nature red in tooth and claw." Indeed, prior to the twentieth-century rationalist and Puritan ideals had numerous points in common, especially among the Anglo-Saxon peoples. For the ideals of progress, of the rational society of liberty, equality, and fraternity, of pure communism, were not originated in the eighteenth century by the rationalistic philosophers of France. As important forces they first came to light in Puritan England of the seventeenth century.[4]

Yet these ideals, especially the purely rationalistic, held within themselves the seeds of their own decay. It is interesting to note that, so far as science was concerned, in spite of its exaltation of human reason there arose, as in religion, an inconsistency between its doctrine and its psychology and practice. It removed man from nature and made him its master by giving him machines and by overestimating the potentialities of his reason; yet in theory it showed his essential connection with and subservience to nature. Man was evolved from animals and was not a special creation of the Deity; furthermore, he might think himself free, but the universal law of causality made it obvious that his every thought and deed was predetermined and that he was as helpless a tool in nature's hands as a drifting cloud. But determinism is a doctrine which self-assertive man has never taken seriously (as witness the Calvinists); it convinces his head but not his heart, and in practice he has to temper it with what Vaihinger calls the philosophy of "as if," for he behaves *as if* he were free. But in the glorification of human reason there was an appeal to his pride, and reason had something to show for itself in steam-engines, factories, medicine, electric power, airplanes, and radio. But the god of reason had some serious reverses, one of the most important of which came out of science itself, as a result of the uncomfortable and searching inquiries of a certain Sigmund Freud into matters connected with the other aspect of scientific discovery—the inseparability of man and nature.

FREUD, ORIGINAL SIN, AND THE UNCONSCIOUS

The rationalists of the nineteenth century were essentially optimists, and it was not surprising that they had no more taste for Freud than for the Church's doctrine of original sin. Their faith in the ideal of progress and the certain triumph of reason was not at all in harmony with Freud's contention that man's highest aspirations had their origin in unconscious forces of a very different character, forces to which he gave such unpleasant names as "incest wishes," "castration complexes," "mother or father fixations," and other phrases of bluntly sexual type. Nor did rationalism take kindly to so irrational an idea as that man's unconscious goal might be to re-enter the womb and revert to a condition of protected irresponsibility, floating blissfully in a warm, sleepy darkness. But Freud's teaching was original sin in a new garb, for it showed the unregenerate Adam behind a thin shell of reason, and if man's highest aspirations were just "rationalizations" of these dark, unconscious forces, did not this go to prove a fundamental doctrine of the Church? Did it not show that man's efforts to save himself by exercise of his unaided will and reason are fruitless? For Humanism and rationalism had altogether neglected a mysterious factor called the Grace of God, believing that the human mind was sufficiently powerful to work out its own salvation. And by the mind they understood merely that aspect of the soul known as intellect.

Now we have seen that intellect is the thinking *machine*; a power drives that machine, but whatever the character of that power the machine can only interpret it in a mechanical way. Therefore when it has to accept an irrational impulse it rationalizes it in the course of putting it into effect. When the unregenerate Adam desires blood just for the sake of blood, the reasoning machine has to find a reasonable purpose for shedding blood, however specious. And it finds it because in many ways the intellect has the most intricately subtle power of adaptation and an almost infinite capacity for self-deception. For it is of immense importance to the self-esteem of the ego that rationalizations should be convincing; otherwise man must admit his failure to stand above nature.

Nevertheless, Freudian doctrine aroused little sympathy until after the Great War when it achieved sudden success, primarily through the ability of its method of psychological healing to cure cases of shell-shock. But the outburst of the unregenerate Adam in the war itself made Freud's ideas much more acceptable, though it is surprising how many intelligent people even to-day will refuse to admit that they have such a thing as an unconscious mind. They regard it as quite an impertinence for anyone to suggest that they do not always know *why* they want what they want and do what they do. Yet they are quite ready to admit that they do not know why their bodies produce such mysterious things as cancers and that they are quite unaware of what is going on in their kidneys, hearts, and bowels. Thus if there are unconscious realms and activities in the body, it seems reasonable to suggest, if only by analogy, that there is an unconscious aspect of the mind.[5]

THE CONTRIBUTION OF JUNG

Analogy might suggest even more than this. The physical body has intimate connections with the entire material universe, most of which are equally unconscious, and might it not be supposed that the unconscious mind extends its roots far beyond the individual, having begun long before he was conceived in the womb? With much more than analogy to support this idea, Freud's pupil C. G. Jung propounded a theory of the unconscious which came close to the fringes of mysticism.[6] For to him the unconscious mind is personal only on its surface; essentially it is collective, racial, and perhaps universal, for Jung found that in their dreams modern men and women spontaneously produced myths and symbols thousands of years old of which they had no conscious knowledge. Thus the infantile sex life of the individual was a comparatively unimportant factor in the unconscious, and Freud's analysis was found to be just the first important step into this undiscovered realm.

The significance of the idea of the unconscious is two-fold, for it reveals a natural universe on the inside of man as well as on the outside. It also raises important questions as to the character of man's real self. I have already suggested that this self lies much deeper than conscious reason and intellect, deeper even than man's individuality which appears more and more to be an instrument animated by natural and universal forces. Now that we find the roots of the soul descending far below the personal level, we can understand why Jung describes the ego (which we ordinarily regard as our central self) as a complex of the unconscious. That is to say, it is a device employed by the unconscious mind to achieve certain results; in the same way the apparently self-contained human body is a device employed by nature to achieve certain results. But it must not be thought that this employment of a device is necessarily purposive in the same way that the reasoned actions of human beings are, for human purpose may be only a rationalization of natural impulse, as reason can only operate in terms of purpose.

To us these ideas are very new. But I said that they bordered on mysticism because in fact they would have been well understood by many of the ancient peoples of the world. Thus to the Hindus man's self was identified with his individual person only because of his limited vision; they knew that if this vision could be enlarged, he would discover that his true self was Brahman. In other words, man's ego is a trick or device (*maya*)[7] to assist the functions of life, for if life is to manifest itself it must do so in the form of separate things. Life as such is one and has no form; nobody has ever seen life without a form. Thus, according to the Vedic teaching of the Hindus, Brahman is one and has in itself no form, and hence Brahman as such cannot do anything, cannot express itself. Action and expression can only be achieved when Brahman manifests itself in these devices or forms, and therefore they say that actions are done by the forms and not by Brahman.

Parallel teachings may be found in other ancient civilizations, notably the Egyptian and Chinese. Thus in the Shabaka inscription of ancient Egypt we find:[8]

Ptah lived as the governor in every body, and as the tongue in every mouth of all the gods, all cattle, all reptiles and everything else. . . . Thus every kind of work and every handicraft, and everything done with the arms, and every motion of the legs, and every action of all the limbs take places through his command, which . . . giveth value to everything.

And the Chinese sage Chuang Tzu writing about 200 B.C. says:[9]

Your body is the delegated image of Tao. Your life is not your own. It is the delegated harmony of Tao. Your individuality is not your own. It is the delegated adaptability of Tao. . . . You move, but know not how. You are at rest, but know not why. . . . These are the operations of the laws of Tao.

Such illustrations might be multiplied indefinitely, and there is every reason to believe that this was not just speculative philosophy. These ancient sages wrote not what they *thought* but what they *felt*, and the intuitive and poetic quality of their wisdom is emphasized by the fact that they simply stated what they felt and seldom, if ever, argued the point.

But modern man demands that his reason be convinced and expects his philosophy to be argued like a proposition in geometry. Among thinking people this is a heritage some five hundred years old at least and neither Freud nor wars and crises will make him doubt the supremacy of reason in a mere thirty years. But this heritage has left him in an awkward position having slain his faith in the psychologically satisfying doctrines of the Church, for there is no doubt that those who can really believe in a loving God, in the redemptive power of His Christ and in the efficacy of confession, penance, and absolution, are essentially happy people. They feel themselves to lie in the everlasting arms of a Father whose demands on them are not too exacting because, having taken on human flesh Himself, He knows its frailties and because, having understood all, He can forgive all. For this and other reasons the Catholic Church is a master in the art of relieving man of his responsibilities, and where its priests do not indulge in petty politics and mild terrorism its people are among the happiest on earth. For they are able to trust life, knowing that however much it may pain them its Master will never let them down.

THE NEW RELIGIONS

But what of those whose reason will not allow them to believe these things? What do they do when the pains of life become too much? The majority, I suppose, try to forget them, and civilization offers countless ways of escape— movies, sports, magazines, mystery novels, high-speed travel and the more time-honored remedies of wine, women, and song, all of which while being instructive, entertaining, and relatively harmless do not really solve the problem. For underlying all and the unescapable, wearing threats of economic insecurity and war, the tense, nerve-wracking struggle of business, the social and economic barriers to normal sex life coupled with the saddest misunderstanding of the art of marriage, the frustration of trying to make oneself a place in a huge, unwieldy community that cares nothing for you—one might compile quite a long list. And to know that the escapes do not work one has just to look at faces, especially when people think they are not being watched.

Then there are those who, being fundamentally religious and yet skeptical of orthodox Christianity, resort to the various new religions with which modern society abounds— Christian Science, Theosophy, Spiritualism, Buchmanism, Rosicrucianism, not to mention those unnamed cults which revolve around such personalities as Krishnamurti, Ouspensky, Meher Baba, Alice Bailey, the Ballards, Gurdjieff, Crowley and a thousand other lesser teachers whose followers are comparatively few but often influential.[10] In the same category must be included those who have found a substitute for religion in one of the many schools of the new psychology, some of which are almost semi-religious in a certain sense of the word. But this category is especially interesting because although the man-in-the-street may have little or no knowledge of such things, they are becoming increasingly popular among the intelligentsia, and in small, unobtrusive ways their influence slowly extends to society as a whole. It has often been observed that members of this category and also of the churches are predominantly women approaching or past the middle of life—a class which seems to constitute a special problem in the modern world. Many were deprived of their husbands in the Great War, others have lost them somewhat early in life for American men in particular are apt to die young through business worries and nervous strain. Others still are those who have failed to marry at all or who have made unsuccessful marriages. Thus it is often concluded that their interest in these matters is simply the result of sexual frustration. But while this may well be a contributory cause in some cases, it should be remembered that people naturally acquire an interest in religion in the latter half of life, having accomplished their mundane duties, and that women are more inclined to religious feeling than men. Perceiving this as a natural phenomenon the Hindus divided life into two main stages. In the first man's duties consisted of Artha and Kama, the fulfillment of the duties of citizenship and the fulfillment of the senses—making a position in the world and establishing a family on the one hand, and the life of love, sex, and æsthetics on the other. When these were completed came the stage of Dharma or devotion to religion.

Apart from the definite adherents of these new religious and "religio-psychological" groups there are innumerable "seekers" who find no one creed fully satisfying, and who drift from group to group, seeking they know not what unless it is that magical knowledge which will solve all problems and set their souls free from fear. Sometimes they think they have almost found it in this or that "ism," but what a strange place to look for the secret of life! Surely it is more likely that this secret will be found in life itself and not in doctrines and ideas *about* life?

> Some look for Truth in creeds and forms and rules;
> Some search for doubts and dogmas in the schools,
> But from behind the Veil a Voice proclaims,
> "Your road lies neither here nor there, O fools!"

For the peculiar thing is that both what we are trying to escape and what we are trying to find are inside ourselves. This, as we have seen, is almost more true of modern man than of the primitive, for our difficulty is what to do with ourselves rather than the external world.

Thus, at the risk of repeating a truism, it is obvious that unless we can come face to face with the difficulty in ourselves, everything to which we look for salvation is nothing more than an extra curtain with which to hide that difficulty from our eyes. Whether salvation is sought in mere forgetting or in a definite attempt to find salvation either through religion, philosophy, or psychological healing the same principle applies. Psychological healing in particular has been devised for the very purpose of enabling man to face himself, to accept nature in himself with all its primeval desires and fears. Oddly enough, however, many of the most fervent devotees of psychology are outstanding examples of its failure to help them. It does not attempt to offer comforting doctrines about this world or the hereafter like many forms of religion and philosophy, nor does it hold out promises of power and success. It digs ruthlessly into the secret places of the heart and drags out man's most carefully guarded mysteries, and yet one has met accredited and fully qualified practitioners of this science who appear to be anything but reconciled to themselves or to life. For it seems that even the acceptance of life can be used as a means to escape it.

THE INSTRUMENT OF FREEDOM

But this is not surprising. The seekers for forgetfulness, salvation, and health of the mind alike want happiness, and therefore among these classes one cannot expect to find happy people. Those who are happy are interested in religion mainly as a means of expressing their gratitude to life and God and of enabling others to see as they do; they are not looking for personal salvation, for they do not think about such things. But how can they enable others to see as they do if it is true that while those who have happiness do not search for it, those who have not cannot find it by seeking?

We have examined something of the meaning of unhappiness, of the war between the opposites in the human soul, of the fear of fear, of man's consequent isolation from nature and of the way in which this isolation has been intensified in the growth of civilization. We have also shown how man is intimately and inseparably connected with the material and mental universe, and that if he tries to cut himself off from it he must perish. In fact, however, he can only cut himself off in imagination, otherwise he would cease to exist, but we have yet to decide whether this elusive thing called happiness would result from acceptance of the fact of man's union with the rest of life. But if this is true we have to discover how such an acceptance may be made, whether it is possible for man to turn in his flight into isolation and overcome the panic which makes him try to swim against the current instead of with it. In the psychological realm this swimming against the current is called repression, the reaction of proud, conscious reason to the fears and desires of nature in man. This raises the further question of whether acceptance of nature involves just a return to the amorality of the beast, being simply a matter of throwing up all responsibility, following one's whims and drifting about on the tide of life like a fallen leaf. To return to our analogy: life is the current into which man is thrown, and though he struggles against it, it carries him along despite all his efforts, with the result that his efforts achieve nothing but his own unhappiness. Should he then just turn about and drift? But nature gave him the faculties of reason and conscious individuality, and if he is to drift he might as well have been without them. It is more likely that he has them to give expression to immeasurably greater possibilities of nature than the animal can express by instinct, for while the animal is nature's whistle, man is its organ.

Even so, man does not like to be put down to the place of an instrument, however grand that instrument may be, for an instrument is an instrument, and an organ does what it is made to do as subserviently and blindly as a whistle. But this is not the only consideration. It may be that man has a wrong idea of what his self is. In the words of the Hindu sage Patanjali, "Ignorance is the identification of the Seer with the instruments of seeing."[11] Certainly man *as instrument* is an obedient tool whether he likes it or not, but it may be that there is something in man which is more than the instrument, more than his reason and individuality which are part of that instrument and which he mistakenly believes to be his true self. And while as an instrument he is bound, as *this* he is free, and his problem is to become aware of it. Finding it, he will understand that in fleeing from death, fear, and sorrow he is making himself a slave, for he will realize the mysterious truth that in fact he is free both to live and to die, to love and to fear, to rejoice and to be sad, and that in none of these things is there any shame. But man rejects his freedom to do them, imagining that death, fear, and sorrow are the causes of his unhappiness. The real cause is that he does not let himself be free to accept them, for he does not understand that he who is free to love is not really free unless he is also free to fear, and this is the freedom of happiness.

The oldest answers in the world to the problem of happiness are found in religion, for the kind of happiness we are considering belongs to the deepest realms of the human spirit. But this should not lead us to suppose that it is something remote from familiar experience, something to be sought out in supernatural spheres far beyond the world which we know through our five senses. The world of the spirit is so often understood in an almost materialistic way, as a locality infinite in space containing things that are eternal in terms of time.[1] It is thought to be a world corresponding in form and substance to our own, save that its forms and substances are constructed of spirit instead of matter, and its operations governed by different laws, for nothing changes—all things are everlasting. To understand the world of the spirit in this way is to make it wholly different from the world in which we live, and when religion is concerned with this kind of spiritualism a great gulf appears between the world of the spirit and the world of everyday experience, contact with the former being possible only in a disembodied condition, as after death, or in a state of consciousness where we acquire a new set of senses, spiritual senses that can perceive things to which material vision is not attuned.

This view of spirituality is so common in religion that many people believe salvation to lie utterly beyond our present life, being something for which earthly existence is only a preparation and which will be inherited either when we have passed beyond the grave or when, even though still living, our thoughts have ascended to a higher sphere so that we are in this world but not of it. It is probable, however, that this idea has arisen because so much religious teaching is presented in the form of allegory; spiritual truths are presented in terms of time and space for purposes of simplification. Heaven and hell are removed in time to the life after death and in place to a *different* world-order; eternity is represented as unending time, which is not eternity but everlastingness. This kind of simplification may have its uses, but in many ways it is an unnecessary complication for the conception has greater value if we think of heaven and hell as here and now, and of eternity as the timeless, eternal Now.

RELIGION AS A DENIAL OF LIFE

However, this is one of the main trends of thought in religion as generally understood, besides which there is yet another believing that spiritual happiness is attainable on earth but in a somewhat utopian and materialistic way. Both of these trends exist in Christianity, some holding that "on this earth we have no continuing home, therefore we seek one to come," and others working for the establishment of the "kingdom of heaven on earth." The Christian holding the former opinion feels that he can never be at home in this world which he regards as a kind of anteroom to the life hereafter, a place of trial and temptation where God tests the fitness of His children to enter His kingdom. At the same time he will thank his Lord for all the blessings of this earth, for the pleasures which give him joy as well as for the pains which give opportunities to learn wisdom. Yet he is not content with those pleasures, and because they are so fleeting he regards them as mere hints of the glories of paradise which shall endure forever and ever.

But in modern Christianity especially there is another element which existed in olden times, though in a different form. An article of the Apostles' Creed is the belief in the resurrection of the body,[2] the belief that the world to come is not only a spiritual state but also a condition of life where the physical world has been recreated by spiritual power. It is said that God will create a new heaven and a new earth, and that "the kingdom of this world shall become the Kingdom of Our Lord and of His Christ." The modern Christian is apt to regard this teaching in rather a different way, for whereas his ancestors viewed it as something which would happen only at the last day when all the dead would rise from their graves, the modern view is rather that the kingdom of heaven on earth is something which man may create by the Grace of God here and now. Hence the increasing interest of the churches in idealistic politics. Morality becomes something to be practiced, not only to insure salvation in the world to come, but to improve the lot of mankind in the world as it is. For Christianity has become linked to the idea of progress, and the churches are the foremost advocates of peace, of social service, and of political and economic justice.

But both among Christians and among followers of other religions there are those who feel that such ideals are rather naive, either because they seem impossible of achievement or else because they do not seem very desirable. Spiritual happiness, as they understand it, has little to do with either material well-being or everlasting glory in a paradise of heavenly music and streets of pure gold. But they share the same suspicion of the world as it is, believing the highest illumination of the spirit unattainable in the flesh or under the particular limitations of the senses which compel us to view life as a transient alternation of pleasure and pain.

For many centuries there has been a tendency of this kind in the religions of the East, of which the most notable example is Hinayana Buddhism—the type of Buddhism with which the West is most familiar. The Hinayana takes the most gloomy view of the world of any religion, and seeks escape from it by the quickest possible means to a state which is not exactly complete annihilation, but a kind of vague, infinite consciousness from which all personality, all sense of individual identity, and all diversity of form have been removed. In this state there is no pain because there is no pleasure, and no death because there is no longer anyone to die. The gist of its teaching is that when you realize that your personal self does not exist, then you are free of suffering, for suffering can arise only when there is a person to suffer. The same may be said of pleasure, with the result that the Hinayana ideal is a state of tastelessness which is held to be the highest attainable bliss.

A similar ideal might be found by a casual examination of the teachings of Hindu Vedanta as expressed in the Upanishads. For it seems as if the supreme aspiration of the Hindu yogin is to become merged into the infinite Brahman, the one reality of which all diverse forms are illusory expressions. In common with the Hinayana Buddhist, he finds the world unsatisfying because of the impermanence of its glories. Therefore he fights against all those things in himself which move him to seek happiness in the pleasures of the world, learning to see the changing forms of life as a web of delusion hiding the face of God. To him all things are God; mountains, trees, rivers, men, and beasts only seem to be what they are because of the limitations of his own senses. Once those limitations are overcome, the world of diverse form vanishes and there remains only the vast and void infinitude of Brahman in whom is eternal rest and bliss.

Such ideas are frequent in Eastern thought, although they do not represent its deepest meaning. To most of us they are abstract and incomprehensible. Nevertheless, countless religious people maintain that the end and aim of our life here on earth is an eternal condition whose characteristics may be described in one of the following ways. First, a state beyond death wherein the beauties of life are greatly magnified and all its pains and limitations overcome. Second, a state in this life wherein earthly pains and limitations have been overcome by the exercise of human reason and skill, inspired by the Grace of God. Third, a state attainable either in the body or out of it where human consciousness has been raised above the limits imposed upon it by the personal self and its five senses, wherein all diversity of form, all pairs of opposites, have been merged into the infinite and formless divine essence from which they originally came.

ABOLISHING THE UNIVERSE

All these three have certain elements in common. There is a distaste for the world as it is, implying that the wrong is not so much in the external world as in one's own imperfect self, which is either doomed to live in this world on account of those imperfections or else which sees that world falsely, being deluded by imperfect senses. There is also the hope for an eternal state in which good things are made permanent or abolished altogether along with the evil. And, most significant of all, there is the implication that one of these religious states is the ultimate purpose of our earthly existence, from which it must follow that appropriate religious activities are fundamentally the only worth-while pursuits for mankind. All other pursuits must therefore be considered subordinate and ephemeral, and in this view art, literature, music, politics, science, drama, exploration, and sport become vain and empty unless they are regarded simply as means of keeping body and soul together in reasonable comfort, or unless they are used for specifically religious purposes. Apart from these two uses they become simply the trimmings of life, the mere gilt on the pill, mere "relaxations" to assuage in as harmless a manner as possible our carnal nature lest its sufferings become too great for us to bear.

The direction of this kind of religion is even more apparent when we consider the various ways and means prescribed for attaining such ideals. Among civilized peoples there are two principal ways of approach to the religious ideal, both of which have various common elements. Both are founded on the idea that the search for spiritual happiness in worldly pleasures is a snare because those pleasures are impermanent; they do, perhaps, impart a certain happiness, but because that happiness is entirely dependent on external circumstances it disappears as soon as those circumstances change. But there is something in man which makes it exceedingly hard for him to avoid the pursuit of earthly pleasures, and this tendency religion attempts to vanquish by a strongly hostile attitude to them. Hence the general antipathy in religion to all that pertains to the senses, and especially to the most elementary and important of earthly pleasures which are to be found in the sexual functions.

The first of the two ways of approach to the religious ideal is found mainly in Christianity. It is the way of mortification of the flesh in order that the eyes may be turned from the snares of the world to the eternal glories of the world beyond. By prayer, fasting, and acts of charity, by abstinence from fleshly delights, man may make himself fit to receive, feel, and rejoice in the Grace of God which senses deluded by earthly things cannot appreciate. If the senses are coarsened by carnal pleasures, man becomes incapable of entering either now or hereafter into that realm of supernatural glory to which the Grace of God belongs. By its light he is not illumined but burned because of his impurities, for only those things which have been refined of all evil can exist within it.

The second way is similar in most respects, save that it is a way of self-development, wherein the individual relies not on God, but on his own power of willing. It is found in Buddhism and Vedanta, and consists of exercises in mortification and meditation whose object is similarly to refine the senses, to turn them away from the snares of the world and finally to root out from the soul the sense of personal identity and self-sufficiency and its desire to find happiness in the forms of life.

Obviously we are discussing some of the more extreme forms of religious theory and practice; generally speaking, their outward forms have been increasingly modified in the course of years. But there has been little change in the underlying philosophy, which amounts virtually to the complete denial of life as we understand it. For according to this kind of teaching the world of the senses has been made for the sole purpose of encompassing the human soul with a variety of snares. Even the "highest" delights of the senses such as are to be found in the arts are "trimmings," and the less refined joys of eating and sex are just tolerated in so far as they are used only for the purpose of maintaining and reproducing life. Today the harsh attitude of religion to these things has been appreciably softened, but this softening is rather a concession to human nature than an attempt to alter the fundamental premises of religious doctrine. And a mere concession to human nature it will remain while so many types of religious philosophy regard the material and spiritual worlds as irreconcilably opposed.

The problem is important because it affects the usefulness of religion to the greater part of mankind. The belief is still generally prevalent that those who wish to "go furthest" in religion must practice extremes of fasting and chastity and other forms of cumbersome discipline to acquire the necessary spiritual sensitivity for making contact with states of consciousness and mystical insight which less refined senses can no more experience than a jaded palate can taste the subtleties of a fine wine. But this refining and exaltation of consciousness by means of asceticism is obviously a vocation for the very few, for even if it were practicable for the majority it would not be altogether desirable to have the world converted into a vast Tibet. It would be wiser to heed the warning of Lucretius, "*Tantum religio potuit suadere malorum,*" or "Too much religion is apt to encourage evil."

But if the highest illumination of the spirit is only attainable by such means, of what use is religion to the ordinary run of mankind? It may encourage them to a greater morality; it may even teach them to love one another, though the course of history does not suggest that there has been much success in this. It may also give them a sense of the reality of a Father God to whom they can pray as "a very present help in time of trouble." But this does not begin to exhaust the possibilities of religion because it comes nowhere near to the real essentials of religion; it scarcely touches what is called "religious experience," without which doctrines, rites, and observances are the emptiest shells. It cannot be assumed that because most religious people are moral, moral people are therefore religious. As Wilde said, "When I am happy I am always good, but when I am good I am seldom happy," and this becomes more true than ever if by happiness we mean the state that arises from religious experience.

THE RELIGIOUS EXPERIENCE

Religious experience is something like artistic or musical inspiration, though inspiration is a word that through misuse has unfortunate associations; religious experience is not "uplift" or flighty emotionalism. Strictly speaking, a composer is inspired when melody emerges from the depths of his mind, how or why we do not know. To convey that melody to others he writes it down on paper, employing a technical knowledge which enables him to name the notes which he hears in his mind. This fact is important: his technical knowledge does not *create* the tune in his mind; it simply provides him with a complicated alphabet, and is no more the source of music than the literary alphabet and the rules of grammar are the sources of men's ideas. If he is writing a symphony he will want to orchestrate his melody, but to do this he does not look up the books on harmony and orchestration to find out what combinations of notes he is advised by the rules to put together. He has heard the

whole symphony in his mind with every instrument playing its independent part, and his knowledge of orchestration and harmony simply enables him to tell which is which.
What music teachers call the "rules" of harmony are just
observations on the harmonies most usually used by such
people as Bach and Beethoven. Bach and Beethoven did not
use them because they were in the rules but because they
liked their sound, and if peoples' tastes change so that they
like other sounds then the old harmonic forms are replaced.
It is necessary for a composer to study harmony in order
that he may be able to identify chords which he hears in
his mind, but he does not use his knowledge to *construct*
chords unless he is a mere imitator of other people. In the
same way, language is used not to create thoughts but to
express them, and mastery of prose does not make a great
thinker.

The spiritual genius works in the same way as the musical genius. He has a wider scope because his technique of
expression, his alphabet, is every possible human activity.
For some reason there arises in his soul a feeling of the most
profound happiness, not because of some special event, but
because of the whole of life. This is not necessarily content-
ment or joy; it is rather that he feels himself completely
united to the power that moves the universe, whatever that
may be. This feeling he expresses in two ways, firstly by
living a certain kind of life, and secondly by translating
his feeling into the form of thoughts and words.

People who have not had this feeling make observations
on his actions and words, and from them formulate the
"rules" of religious morality and theology. But this involves
a strange distortion, for as a rule the observer goes about
his work in the wrong way. When the mystic says, "I feel

united with God," the observer is interested primarily in the statement as a revelation of the existence of God, and goes on to consult the mystic's other sayings to find out what kind of God this is and in what manner He behaves. He is interested only secondarily in the mystic's feeling as a feeling, and it occurs to him only as an after thought that it might be possible for himself to feel united with God. Whereat he proceeds to achieve this by trying to think in the same way as the mystic; that is to say, he takes the mystic's *ideas* and substitutes them for his own. He also tries to behave in the same way, imitating the mystic's actions. In other words, he tries to perform a kind of sympathetic magic, and in imitating the mystic's external forms deceives himself and others into thinking that he is really like him. But the important thing about the mystic was his feeling, not his ideas and actions, for these were only reflections of the feeling, and a reflection existing without a light is a sham. Therefore just as great technical proficiency will not make a creative genius in music, morality, theology, and discipline will not make a genius in religion, for these things are results of religious experience, not causes, and by themselves can no more produce it than the tail can be made to wag the dog.

THE SPIRITUAL IRRELEVANCE OF OCCULTISM

This is not the only example of confused thought in searching for religious experience. The other, which we have already mentioned, is the opposition made between the spiritual and the material. Much depends, of course, on the precise meaning given to the word "spirit," but it should certainly not be confused with the word "psychic" and many things described as spiritual are clearly psychic.

There is no definite rule as to how these words should be used, so to be explicit we have to make our own rules. And the spiritual, in the sense in which it is used here, is no more opposed to the material than white is opposed to long. The opposite of white is black, and of long, short; white things are no more necessarily short than material things are unspiritual. But we can say that the material and the psychic are opposed, if only in the sense that they are opposite ends of the same stick. Psychic things belong to the world explored by occultism and "psychic science"—telepathy, clairvoyance, mind-reading, and all those phenomena which appear to require sixth or seventh senses whose development seems unquestionably to be assisted by ascetic practices. The so-called spiritual realms inhabited by departed souls, angels, elementals, and demons, and the source of beatific visions, would be most correctly described as psychic if we are to allow that such things have actual, objective existence. And this world is the logical opposite of the material world because it belongs in the same category; it contains forms and substances, even though its substance may be of a wholly different order from what we understand as matter. People who are in touch with this world, however, are not necessarily spiritual people; they may have unusual faculties of perception and be familiar with the beings and ways of a more glorious world than our own, but this is a matter of *faculty* and *knowledge*, not of spirituality. The technique of living employed by such people is more highly evolved than that of ordinary men, just as the technique of the opera is more complicated than that of pure drama. Opera involves not only acting but singing, playing music, and sometimes dancing, but this does not make it a greater art.

Spirituality belongs in the same category as happiness and freedom, and strictly speaking there is no such thing as the spiritual *world*. If psychic people are to be believed, there is a psychic *world*, and because it is a world entry into it is simply an enlargement of experience. But experience as such never made anyone either free or happy, and in so far as freedom and happiness are concerned with experience the important thing is not experience itself but what is learned from it. Some people learn from experience and others do not; some learn much from a little, others learn little from much. "Without going out of my house," said the Chinese sage Lao Tzu, "I know the whole universe." For the spiritual is in no way divided from the material, nor from the psychic, nor from any other aspect of life. To find it, it is not necessary to go from one state of consciousness to another, from one set of senses to another or from one world to another. Such journeying about in the fields of experience takes you neither toward it nor away from it. In the words of the Psalmist:[3]

Whither shall I go from Thy spirit? Or whither shall I flee from Thy presence?

If I ascend up into heaven, Thou art there: if I make my bed in hell, behold, Thou art there.

If I take the wings of the morning, and dwell in the uttermost parts of the sea; even there shall thy hand lead me, and thy right hand shall hold me.

If I say, Surely the darkness shall cover me; even the night shall be light about me.

Yea, the darkness hideth not from Thee; but the night shineth as the day: the darkness and the light are both alike to Thee.

In fact the spiritual world, if we must use the term, is this world and all possible worlds, and spiritual experience is what we are experiencing at this moment and at any moment—if we look at it in the right way.

UNION WITH LIFE

This is the difference between religious or spiritual experience and artistic inspiration; both are analogous, but the latter is particularized. The artist or musician has a special type of creative genius; he creates pictures or music, for his genius is a specialized gift. But the spiritual genius is not a specialist, for he does not just paint or compose creatively: he *lives* creatively, and his tools are not confined to brush, pen or instrument; they are all things touched by his hand. This is not to say that when he takes up a brush he can paint like Leonardo or that when he takes hammer and chisel he can work like a master-mason. Spiritual experience involves neither technical proficiency nor factual knowledge; it is no short-cut to things that must ordinarily be mastered by pains and practice. Nor is spiritual experience necessarily expressed in any *particular* mode of life; its presence in any given individual cannot be judged by measurement in accordance with certain standards. It can only be felt intuitively, for creative living is not always outwardly distinguishable from any other kind of living; in fact, spiritual people are often at pains to appear as normal as possible. At the same time, although spiritual people may do exactly the same things as others, one feels that their actions are in some way different. There is a story of a Buddhist sage who was about to speak to his disciples when he found that he wanted more light. He pointed to a curtain covering one of the windows and instantly two of the disciples went and rolled it up, whereat the sage remarked, "One of them is right, but the other is wrong."[4]

In itself, spirituality is purely an inner experience; it has no necessary effect whatsoever on one's outward behavior judged from the standards of efficiency and worldly-wisdom. This is not to say, however, that it is something absolutely private and personal, finding no expression that others can see. For spirituality is a deep sense of inner freedom based on the realization that one's self is in complete union and harmony with life, with God, with the Self of the universe or whatever that principle may be called. It is the realization that that union has existed from all time, even though one did not know it, and that nothing in all the world nor anything that oneself can do is able to destroy it. It is thus the sense that the whole might of the universe is at work in one's every thought and action, however trivial and small. In fact this is true of all men and all things, but only the spiritual man really knows it and his realization gives a subtly different quality to his life; all that he does becomes strangely alive, for though its outward appearance is perhaps the same as before it acquires a new meaning. It is this which other people notice, but if he has the gift for teaching they will see it in other ways as well. By his words as well as his deeds and his personal "atmosphere" they will understand that this realization has awakened in him a tremendous love for life in all its aspects.

Prose and the logic of philosophy cannot explain this love; one might as well try to describe a beautiful face by a mathematical account of its measurements and proportions. It is a mixture of the joy of freedom, a childlike sense of wonder, and the inner sensation of absolute harmony with life as in the rhythm of an eternal dance such as the Hindus portray in the interlocked figures of Shiva and his bride.[5] In one sense you feel that your life is not lived by you at all; the power of the universe, fate and destiny, God Himself, are directing all your motions and all your responsibilities are blown to the winds. In another sense you feel free to move as you wish; you seem to be moving life with the same vast power with which life moves you, and your littlest acts become filled with gigantic possibilities. Indeed, physicists tell us that the stars are affected when we lift a single finger. The result of these two feelings is that you no longer distinguish between what you do to life and what life does to you; it is as if two dancers moved in such perfect accord that the distinction between lead and response vanished, as if the two became one and the same motion. By the whirling, ever changing movement of this dance you are carried along without pause, but not like a drunken man in a torrent, for you as much as life are the source of the movement. And this is real freedom; it includes both freedom to move and to be moved; action and passivity are merged, and in spirituality as well as in marriage this is the fulfillment of love.

THE SPIRITUALITY OF EVERYDAY LIFE

All this, however, does not take place in the ecstasy of trance, in some abstract state of consciousness where all shapes and substances have become merged into a single infinite essence. The spiritual man does not perform his ordinary activities as one in a dream, letting his surface thoughts and deeds run on mechanically. He can become just as much absorbed in the usual affairs of the world as anyone else, but in a certain way he sanctifies them for under his hands sharpening a pencil becomes as much a religious act as prayer or meditation. Indeed, he can afford to become absorbed in everyday affairs almost more than others, and he can do so with a certain zest and abandon for to him ordinary human thoughts and activities are as much included in the dance of the spirit as is anything else. This, indeed, is much of his secret, for he knows that spirituality does not consist in thinking always about the spiritual as such. His world is not divided into "water-tight compartments" and his religion is not a special form of thought and activity, for the spiritual and the material are not separated.

But because a man does not occupy himself with the ordinary pursuits of mankind, this is no indication that he lacks spiritual understanding. He is free to follow whatever occupation he pleases—monk, philosopher, lawyer, clerk, or tradesman, but from the spiritual point of view a priest is not necessarily more holy than a truck-driver. Furthermore, to obtain spiritual experience it is not essential to "vex your mournful minds with pious pains," to spend years in the study of theology, to retire from the world, to become a vegetarian and teetotaler, to practice mental acrobatics and seek out "higher realms" of consciousness, to abstain from sexuality, or to develop such peculiar gifts as "fourth-dimensional vision." Certainly these things are necessary for the professional philosopher or for that particular type of *scientist* whose field of research is the psychic world. If we are going to find out how our present senses may be developed, how we can tap sources of nervous energy as yet unused, how we can understand time in terms of space and see past and future at once, how we can transfer thought or how we can acquire the faculty of immovable concentration, then indeed we have to go in training even more rigorously than the professional athlete. To acquire psychic faculties you must practice just as much as if you wanted to hold the world's record for sprinting or to be able to walk on hot coals without being burned.

THE NONESSENTIALS OF RELIGION

Religion as we understand it includes many things which do not strictly belong to it, because in olden times it had to fulfill functions which have now been taken over by scientists, doctors, and lawyers. At one time the major preoccupation of so-called religion was the study and manipulation of the unknown and the unseen; as these things become known and seen they passed out of the hands of priests. But when priests were considered the wisest of all men they were expected to have answers to all the problems which others did not understand. They were expected to know the causes of disease, the behavior and influence of the stars, the origin of such natural phenomena as thunder, storms, and famines, not to mention the more remote questions of what happens after death and whether there are gods and angels.

Many of these problems have now been taken over by science, though we are still ignorant of the life after death and still have no objective evidence of the existence of "supernatural" beings. Therefore the priests are still the authorities on such matters even though they remain legitimate objects of scientific inquiry and have no essential connection with religion. The day may come when science, physical or psychic, will be able to answer these questions, and some scientists imagine that there will then be no further need for religion, having no clear idea of what religion is. This is not exactly their fault, for religious people seldom understand the true function of religion and still waste thought and energy in a war with science based on wholly false premises.

If it could be proved objectively and scientifically that there was a life after death and that supernatural beings do exist this would have about as much religious significance as the discovery of a new continent, of the existence of life on Mars, or of the uses of electricity. It would be neither more nor less than an addition to human experience and knowledge. It would not necessarily be an addition to human wisdom, and this is the province of religion. For wisdom is not factual knowledge nor mere quantity and range of experience, nor even facility in the use of knowledge and experience. Wisdom is a quality of the psychological or spiritual relationship between man and his experience. When that relationship is wise and harmonious man's experiences set him free, but when it is unwise and discordant his experiences bind him.

Religion alone can deal with that relationship, and this is its essential function. For what do we find left in religion when its *quasi*-scientific aspect is removed? There is the whole, vast problem of love or spiritual union which is contained in the question, "How can I learn to love life, whose source and essence we call God? How can I learn to be united with it in all its expressions, in living and dying, in love and fear, in the outer world of circumstances and in the inner world of thought and feeling, so that in union with it I may find freedom?" Now science cannot teach any kind of love, not even the love between man and woman, for who ever learned to love his wife out of a psychological textbook on matrimony? Morality, which religion would teach as having supernatural sanctions, is just the expression of love; it follows it as a consequence and does not precede it as a cause. The will of God as expressed in morality is not a ukase which we should merely obey, for the purpose of His will is not that there should be morality, but that there should be love, and morality is just the "outward and visible sign of an inward and spiritual grace."

In so far as religion has diverged from its main purpose into psychism, morality for its own sake, speculative theology, concern for the life after death, and attempts to awaken spirituality by imitating its expressions, it has also put itself out of touch with people who have no desire to be religious specialists. Those who cannot feel that man's principal concern should lie outside this world, who feel that salvation has nothing to do with removal to another realm of experience or with mere obedience to a moral law —such people can find little assistance from religion as usually taught, and to-day they constitute a very large proportion of intelligent men and women. For the nineteenth-century conflict between religion and science was, for those whose eyes were open, a stripping-off of nonessentials from religion, but unfortunately official religion seldom saw it in this way. It clung to supernaturalism, which, rightly or wrongly, rationalist science had discredited, and continued to make it the keystone of spirituality.

But this kind of religion does not encourage the type of love upon which spirituality is founded. We have seen that its technique is imitative and thus unlikely to produce genuine, first-hand religious experience; we have also seen that its contempt of this world and its concentration on the life hereafter has little to do with the essentials of religion. This is not all, for not only has it little to do with such essentials; it is also a decided hindrance to spiritual growth because it encourages a "love" of God on a false basis. God is loved not because He has given us *this* world, but because He is said to have promised a much better world in the life after death. His gift to us of this world is therefore declined without thanks—an effrontery which is softened by describing this world as a place of trial for fitness to enter the world to come, on the principle that if you refuse God's first gift, you will get His second.

THE "HIGHER SENSUALITY"

But if God created this world only as a temporary place of trial, He seems to have taken a wholly unnecessary amount of trouble in its construction. He gave us senses which as yet we have hardly begun to develop to their full potentialities, and yet religion warns us against those senses as if they were given us simply as a sop to embellish life with such superficial trimmings as art, literature, music, and athletics so that in playing with them we may have a little relaxation from the more important task of fitting ourselves for the hereafter. But there is a way of looking at things whereby these "trimmings" become the main business of life, and religion the means to their fulfillment, on the principle that religion was made for life and not life for religion. For the contempt of the world of the senses is peculiarly like the fable of the sour grapes. Man burned his fingers at the game of pleasure, and instead of learning to play it aright was filled with fear and relegated pleasure to the realms of the Devil and his vanities, crying:

> The earthly hope men set their hearts upon
> Turns ashes, or it prospers, and anon,
>   Like snow upon the Desert's dusky face,
> Lighting a little hour or two, is gone.

But the whole point about the beauties of the earth is

that they would be intolerable if they did not change and vanish. A woman is not less beautiful and desirable because she grows old and white; if she had eternal youth she would be a monster, as many women are who refuse to accept the different beauties of old age and death. For the beauty of life is not in any one of its stages but in the whole movement from birth to death, and if this movement is in any way resisted or interrupted there come unhappiness, maladjustment and neurotic disease. Those who look pitiful and hideous in their old age are only so because years rankle them, because they have not accepted the rhythm of their life and go forward to old age with regretful glances behind at lost glories.

Certainly all pleasures are transient; otherwise we should cease to appreciate them, but if this be made the excuse for refusing to enjoy them, one must suspect that man's ideas of happiness are horribly confused. The secret of the enjoyment of pleasure is to know when to stop. Man does not learn this secret easily, but to shun pleasure altogether is cowardly avoidance of a difficult task. For we have to learn the art of enjoying things *because* they are impermanent. We do this every time we listen to music. We do not seize hold of a particular chord or phrase and shout at the orchestra to go on playing it for the rest of the evening; on the contrary, however much we may like that particular moment of music, we know that its perpetuation would interrupt and kill the movement of melody. We understand that the beauty of a symphony is less in these musical moments than in the whole movement from beginning to end. If the symphony tries to go on too long, if at a certain point the composer exhausts his creative ability and tries to carry on just for the sake of filling in the required space of time, then we begin to fidget in our chairs, feeling that he has denied the natural rhythm, has broken the smooth curve from birth to death and that though a pretense at life is being made it is in fact a living death.

THE PROBLEM OF PAIN

But by itself this philosophy of "higher sensuality" is inadequate, for life is not like a musical masterpiece in certain respects. We may find all of a musical masterpiece beautiful; from the sensual point of view life is only beautiful in parts; it has also ugliness, pain, and horror, and hence the love for a God who will remove these things in the world to come. But this, too, is an avoidance of the problem. For the attitude of ordinary religion to both the pleasures and the pains of this world is negative. Pleasure is suspected, and in the everlasting life pain is not.

But we must now ask whether it is not possible that greater heights of spirituality may be attained by a positive attitude to pleasure and pain in this world. If this is possible, it is clear that religion has no special concern with the life after death and that spirituality has nothing whatever to do with retiring from this world. No one can deny the existence of a life after death, but that it should be a more spiritual life than this one is a wholly unreasonable assumption. If it is true that we are physically reincarnated on this earth or another, the whole picture is changed. But if orthodox Christianity is right in its belief that we have only one material life, then the next life will be psychic because according to our definition there can be no such thing as a spiritual world, spirituality being a quality of life and not a kind of existence in the same category as the material and the psychic.

Spirituality is therefore a way of living in whatever world one happens to be, and is in no way separable from the actual process of living in that world. In other words, there is no difference between religion and ordinary, everyday life; religious ideas and practices (which are no more religion itself than any other activities) exist solely to promote a positive and loving attitude toward ordinary life and what it stands for, namely, God. Unless one happens to be a religious specialist, which is not necessarily the same thing as a spiritual person, religious practices are not ends in themselves. They are means to a fuller and greater life *in this world*, involving a positive and constructive attitude to pleasure and pain alike, and thus an increasing ability to learn happiness and freedom from every possible kind of experience. In this sense, religion is union with life; whether that life is this present life of physical form, of thought and feeling with brain and soul, or whether it is a future life of purely psychic substance is beside the point. These are only different grades of existence; they are not different grades of spirituality, for the same spiritual laws apply in every grade of existence, and when one has learned union with one of them, one has discovered the secret of union with any of them.

We have suggested that the secret of this union lies in a positive attitude toward the world in which we live. To repeat the question which religion has to answer, we want to discover how we can learn to be united with life in all its expressions, in living and dying, in love and fear, in the outer world of circumstance and in the inner world of thought and feeling, so that in union with it we may find freedom and happiness. To be united with life in all its expressions may seem a large demand to make on oneself, for those expressions include disease, pain, death, madness, and all the horrors which man can devise, wittingly or unwittingly, for his fellow-creatures. In fact the "nub" of the whole problem is the acceptance of the dark side of life, for this is the very occasion of our unhappiness. "Acceptance" may seem a weak word for a positive attitude of love, but it is used because the type of love in question is relaxed. It is positive but not aggressive; it grows in its own way and is not forced. Therefore we may say that it is not enough to *tolerate* the dark side of life; acceptance in this sense is much more than a "let it be" with a resigned shrug of the shoulders. Let us call it "creative acceptance," though because this phrase smacks overmuch of philosophical jargon we will write the noun and only remember its qualifying adjective. This is perhaps wise in another way, for a truth oddly comes out of a play on words: to be genuine, acceptance must be unqualified.

3 · THE WAY OF ACCEPTANCE

In recent years men seem to have discovered a new virtue and a new vice in the human soul. The virtue is called "accepting life," and the vice "escaping from life"—two phrases whose meaning, from a strictly philosophical point of view, is most doubtful. The phrases themselves were apparently brought into popularity and given special significance, however vague, by the new movement in psychology which began with Freud, being continued by Adler, Jung, and a thousand others. Of course, neither the virtue nor the vice is new, and psychologists were not the first to become aware of them. Carlyle spoke of them as the "Everlasting Yea" and the "Everlasting Nay," and though modern psychology has perhaps investigated them with a newer and bolder thoroughness, they have been known throughout history under a hundred different names.

But, save for some isolated instances, the idea of accepting life as understood in modern psychology has been noticeably absent from the philosophy and religion of the Western World. For centuries the symbol of Christian moral endeavor has been St. Michael and the Dragon—St. Michael standing triumphant on the dying body of a villainous clawed and winged serpent, his spear driven into its heart. That serpent was a symbol not only of greed, hatred, lust, and ignorance but of all that is involved in the trinity of "the world, the flesh and the devil." At the risk of quoting something that most people know by heart, it is interesting to turn in this connection to the fifth chapter of St. Matthew's Gospel.

> But I say unto you, That ye resist not evil: but whosoever shall smite thee on thy right cheek, turn to him the other also. . . . Ye have heard that it hath been said, Thou shalt love thy neighbour, and hate thine enemy. But I say unto you, Love your enemies, . . . That ye may be the children of your Father which is in heaven: for he maketh his sun to rise on the evil and on the good, and sendeth rain on the just and on the unjust.

Christian psychology makes an interesting distinction between the man himself and the evil in him. In accordance with the above precepts the man himself, the immortal soul, is to be loved. But for that very love and for the eternal salvation of that soul, the evil in him is to be fought, hated, and slain without quarter. Yet it is questionable whether Jesus had just that idea in mind. Certainly he was referring to what one's reaction should be to evil treatment from other people, but it is possible, even probable, that the words "resist not evil" carry more meaning than that. It is likely that he told men to love their enemies not only because their enemies were human, but also because love is the only wise reaction to evil of any kind, whether human, natural, or demonic.

An earlier myth than that of St. Michael and the Dragon tells of an encounter with a monster who for every one head slashed off by the hero's sword grew seven new heads. Indeed, the problem of evil is not quite so straightforward as the accepted technique of "morality-by-battle" would assume. Those desires, feelings, and impulses in the soul which are called evil seem to thrive on resistance because resistance belongs to their own nature, and, as the Buddha said, "Hatred ceases not by hatred alone; hatred ceases but by love." This seems reasonable enough when applied to persons, but somehow we find it difficult to believe that the impulse of hate can only be overcome by loving it. But, as with fear, the hate of hatred is only adding one hate to another, and its results are as contrary as those of the war which was fought to end war. And yet, if you take a gun and shoot a murderer, the result seems to be clear and satisfactory: a dangerous person, who might have killed innocent and defenseless people, has ceased to exist. Should it not be equally satisfactory when by violence we remove evil from our minds? If it thereby ceases to exist why should we question the means used to remove it?

To-day this is not quite so much of a problem as it was to some of our ancestors, for now there is a general inclination to regard as evil only the more extreme vices with which the hearts of normal men are little troubled. Many things that the Puritan would have called deadly sins are now either "natural" or positively "healthy." But the problem still exists because Satan has assumed a new form. He cannot terrify and ensnare us so thoroughly as of old with our own "fleshly desires," so he has shifted the emphasis of evil to pain, disease, war, and insecurity—adversaries which we now fight and hate as much as our ancestors fought and hated incontinence, gambling, drunkenness, and irreligion. In one way Satan has the better of us, because whereas our ancestors recognized the evil as something existing inside themselves, something for which each man was personally responsible, we tend to externalize it and make nature or other people responsible. No one (unless a Christian Scientist) need shame himself because of pain and disease; war is the fault, conveniently enough, of Nazis, Fascists, or Communists, and insecurity of an economic system.

The Uses of "Evil"

Nevertheless, there is now among us a section of opinion which not only recognizes the internal origin of all kinds of evil, but which also believes that they are best controlled by a pacifist technique. Needless to say, the leaders of this section of opinion are the psychologists, for in their view any attempt to root out a thought or desire from the mind only results in "repressing" it. Repression in this sense is the forceful damming-up of a psychological urge, which continues to pile up against the barrier until either the barrier breaks or the urge finds another way out. Psychologists do not believe that such urges can ever be wholly eliminated because they arise from an aspect of man's being over which his conscious mind and reason have no real control. This aspect—the unconscious—is irrational nature in man, which centuries of civilization and moral discipline have made him forget or ignore. We know from ordinary, everyday experience of nature that natural forces are exceedingly difficult to check; they can only be redirected. You cannot simply remove the River Amazon, and if you dam it the pressure of water against the dam will constantly increase until the dam breaks or the river overflows its banks—unless you provide an outlet. This is true of almost every little stream as well as of great waterways. In the same way, everyone who has a garden knows that if you want a hedge to grow more vigorously, you must cut it back. Of course, if you tear it up by the roots it will certainly stop growing, but the human soul is not quite like a flower-bed in *that* respect.

We cannot exterminate our own evils any more than the earth can throw out its weeds. But weeds have not choked all those parts of the earth where nature has been left to her own devices; it is only when man interferes with nature that he begins to notice the inconvenient persistence of certain lowly plants to which he gives the name of weeds. Yet even the best-regulated gardens have to have their soil filled with manure and other "unpleasant" fertilizers, and what is true of the soil is also true of the human mind. Where the roses of virtue bloom in their glory there will certainly be a bed of manure; it will be kept in its place, to be sure, but it will certainly be there. This is not said in cynicism, because the "filthiness" of the soil in no way detracts from the beauty of the flower except in the imaginations of those who would like to see roses blooming in mid-air, whose oversensitive tastes are revolted by the realities of nature. However, the expert and enthusiastic gardener finds something almost pleasurable in manure; certainly he does not smear it all over the plants, but a soil well mixed with it he calls "good" and "rich"—not "foul" and "putrid."

This gives us a clew to what is meant by the acceptance of evil, which was never intended to be an excuse for unbridled license. It means that what morality calls evil is a natural urge that no one need fear if it is kept in its proper place—in the ground. In other words, if you find yourself thinking that you want to murder someone, to commit adultery, to rob a bank or beat your wife, don't try to force the thought away. Forcing the thought away increases its power until it demands expression in action. On the other hand, there are times when people become obsessed with such thoughts, even if they have never tried to resist them.

The thought takes hold of their imaginations with an apparently autonomous and irresistible power and drives them to the deed; this is precisely what the moralist fears. Yet Berdyaev writes in his *Freedom and the Spirit*:[1]

Our attitude towards evil must be free from hatred, and has itself need to be enlightened in character. . . . Satan rejoices when he succeeds in inspiring us with diabolical feelings to himself. It is he who wins when his own methods are turned against himself. . . . A continual denunciation of evil and its agents merely encourages its growth in the world—a truth sufficiently revealed in the Gospels, but to which we remain persistently blind.

These words are significant from a philosopher of the Catholic Church. For those Christians who have really studied the New Testament know as well as psychologists that evil is not overcome by violence; but apparently those who would inculcate morality by forceful, legalistic discipline have never troubled to read St. Paul. If there is any doubt about the words of Christ, there can be no two opinions about the following passage from the Epistle to the Romans:[2]

For when we were in the flesh, the motions of sins, which were by the law, did work in our members to bring forth fruit unto death. . . . What shall we say then? Is the law sin? God forbid, Nay, I had not known sin, but by the law: for I had not known lust except the law had said, Thou shalt not covet. But sin, taking occasion by the commandment, wrought in me all manner of concupiscence. For without the law sin was dead. For I was alive without the law once: but when the commandment came, sin revived, and I died.

What was St. Paul's alternative? This is given perhaps most clearly in the Epistle to the Galatians. In his own mystical terminology it is that Christ must be born in the human soul so that the will of Christ shall supplant human will. Laws and rules will then be irrelevant because whatever the individual desires to do will be the desire of Christ. We have to discover just exactly what this means, but it will immediately be clear that as Christ means love it will involve a new attitude to evil.[3]

St. Michael as the Dragon

But there is an important point which is often overlooked. We described a certain attitude to evil as pacifistic, and a pacifist is often one who hates the hating of hatred—three hates instead of one!—a fact which explains the frequently violent intolerance of peace propagandists. For St. Michael is as much an integral part of the human soul as evil itself, and unless the St. Michael urge of impatience with evil and pain is accepted along with evil and pain, the acceptance is only one-sided.[4] This is indeed a point on which the new psychology has to be careful lest in becoming reconciled with one devil it create another in the form of St. Michael himself. The phrase "acceptance of life" means precisely the acceptance of the *whole* of life, and should certainly not be understood as mere spiritual laissez faire. Thus the spiritual ideal is more than "a wise passiveness"—a partial attitude that excludes force and effort, that accepts old evils but creates a new one that is almost worse than the old because it is more subtle and complex.

The difficulty of the whole psychology of acceptance is that unless it is understood in the right way it leads into a mental labyrinth whose fine nuances take us further and further from realities. There is no doubt that the technique of relaxation or acceptance "works" where an aggressive attitude would only create further trouble. Everyone who has practiced jujutsu has had a convincing, physical demonstration of the way in which force can be overcome by yielding, by arranging things so that his opponent defeats himself by his own effort. But there are two kinds of acceptance, one which is applied to particular things and the other which is applied to life in general. In exactly the same way there are the two kinds of happiness, one which is occasioned by particular things or events, and the other by the whole of life. The first type of acceptance is a question of *technique* and the second of *spirituality*; there are specific ways to achieve the former, but the latter is strangely elusive.

ACCEPTANCE, PARTIAL AND TOTAL

Jujutsu is an example of the first kind of acceptance, being simply the exchange of one technique of fighting for another. It is therefore an *exclusive* technique just as the technique of psychology is exclusive in that it creates a new "evil" called escapism as the opposite of acceptance. Thus we have these two psychological states called "acceptance of life" and "escape from life," but when they are opposed to one another in this way it is clear that "life" can have only a limited meaning. It means particular things in life— specific evils, desires, events, and situations, because when life is understood in its widest sense there is no possibility of escape from it. Everything is life, even escapism, and if the whole of life is to be accepted the desire to escape must not be made into a new devil. Therefore partial acceptance is what Oriental philosophers would describe as a dualistic as distinct from a non-dualistic state of mind. For according to Hindu and Buddhist teachings the enlightened man attains a state of mind that is one with Brahman or Tathata,[5] the Reality of life which includes all possible things and apart from which nothing exists. This state is non-dualistic because it is union with something to which nothing can be opposed, and in this sense it is complete and absolute acceptance of life, philosophically described as union with the principle that is the meaning, essence, and raison d'être of the universe. In this state man is supremely happy because even though he may be involved in a conflict with pain and evil, even though he may feel the very human emotions of fear, anger, and love, he lives his life with a whole-heartedness and abandon born of the understanding that all things are fundamentally acceptable. For to him there is meaning and divinity in every aspect of the universe and in both the greatness and the littleness, the love and the fear, the joy and the sorrow, and the content and discontent of the human soul. For the Upanishads say:[6]

The Soul is Brahman, the Eternal. It is made of consciousness and mind: It is made of life and vision. It is made of the earth and the waters: It is made of air and space. It is made of light and darkness: It is made of desire and peace. It is made of anger and love: It is made of virtue and vice. It is made of all that is near: It is made of all that is afar. It is made of all.

But this total acceptance and love of life eludes us because in striving to attain it we are constantly at war with that which appears to go against it. The reason is that in trying to be united with life we are striving to achieve something that already exists; the result is that our very efforts to achieve it are hindrances in that they encourage the feeling that we are divorced from life and have to make ourselves one with it. But we cannot realize all at once that this union already exists because centuries of civilization have orphaned us from nature both in and around us, making us feel that we are self-contained, independent, and autonomous egos. The primitive does not feel this to the same extent, having what Levy-Brühl described as a *participation mystique* with nature, which is to say a union of which he is not fully aware because he has never been conscious of what it means to be separated from nature. That feeling of separation must come before union can have its full meaning for us. Thus in the parable of the Prodigal Son it is the returning prodigal for whom the fatted calf is slain—not the faithful son who had always stayed at home and had never been separated from his father.

Thus if man is to realize again his fundamental unity and harmony with life he must proceed by the roundabout way of trying to get that which he already has until he convinces himself of his own folly. For it is only by *trying* to accept life as a whole that we can make ourselves aware that there was never any real need to try, and that spirituality is in fact a matter of "becoming what we are." In trying actively to accept life we find that this is successful only in regard to particular things; we reconcile ourselves to the dark side of life only to find that we are not reconciled to our desire to escape from it, and this desire in itself is an aspect of that dark side. By this method something is always left out of the whole, with the result that our acceptance and therefore our happiness is still dependent on particular things, and we are just as far from including the whole as ever. For this reason a large number of psychological patients are never really cured. Specific neuroses of the more obvious kind are certainly overcome, but except in some rare cases the great happiness remains undiscovered. This is not at all surprising, for not only is total acceptance the most elusive thing in the world; it is also something against which intellect and reason rebel.

THE THREE STAGES OF MORALITY

It is argued that if the highest spirituality is simply a matter of accepting life *as it is*, and if this is something which we already have but do not realize, then its attainment will make no difference whatever to our lives. It may possibly make us inwardly happy, but if this is not expressed outwardly in different and better thoughts and actions, it is of no real value. Moreover, the idea of a supreme Reality or God that is manifested alike by *all* forms of life is amoral and dangerous, and is at variance with the important Christian doctrine that the world-order is basically a moral order. But this view of spirituality is only inconsistent with a moral world-order in so far as the morality in question is the invention of human intellect and wishful thinking. If, however, the foundation of morality is "to love your neighbor as yourself," it cannot be said that total acceptance is inconsistent with a moral world-order. For it involves acceptance of the virtues and vices of other people as much as of one's own. More than this, although the idea suggests amorality, it seldom works out this way in practice—a paradox that will subsequently be clear when we consider total acceptance in detail.[7]

But it should be noted that there is an important difference between those whose acceptance is partial and those whose acceptance is total. The ordinary moralist feels that he is not free to be anything but moral; in other words, he feels *compelled* to be moral—for a variety of reasons. It may be that he fears the wrath of God or the pangs of conscience; it may be that he has an egotistic sense of duty, thinking that his own and other people's natures *ought* to conform with the dictates of his reason. But he is slavishly moral, and he fights his "lower nature" because he is either too afraid or too proud to do anything else. As to those whose acceptance is partial, they do not feel free to fight their lower nature; they think that they ought to accept it because anything else would be escaping from life. The result is that they make a compulsive discipline out of psychological relaxation and so "exchange King Stork for King Log." But to accept totally is to be *free* to be moral, and he who follows a moral law in freedom does not suffer the consequences of repression in the same way as the slavish moralist. Part of the secret of this freedom is that he knows he is also free to be immoral, for St. Michael and the Dragon are given equal recognition. In practice, however, free people are seldom immoral because the Dragon no longer impresses them with his forbidden glamour; they find preoccupation with evil merely tedious for reasons which will later be apparent. To quote Berdyaev again:[8]

> The exaggeration of the power of temptation can hardly be a positive means of overcoming it. . . . As long as in our struggle against evil we regard it as strong and enticing, and at the same time both awe-inspiring and forbidden, we are not going to achieve any radical or final victory over it . . . it will remain invincible as long as it is so regarded. . . . The attraction of evil is a lie and an illusion. . . . Only the knowledge of its absolute emptiness and tedium can give us the victory over it.

CHRISTIANITY AND ORIENTAL RELIGION

In Christianity the idea of total acceptance is somewhat hidden; it is only spoken of directly in some of the writings of the mystics, but it is soon discovered when we begin to make a thorough search into the symbolism of Christian doctrine. In the religions of the East, however, it is given particular emphasis; in fact, it is the fundamental principle of Vedantist, Buddhist, and Taoist philosophy. The chief difference between these Eastern religions and Christianity is that, on the surface at least, Christianity is concerned with belief in doctrines whereas the Eastern religions are concerned with states of mind. That is to say, Christianity tends to be a theological and ethical religion, while Buddhism, Taoism, and Vedanta are psychological religions. In Christianity the supreme attainment is reserved for the life after death and it is seldom described in more definite terms than "the bliss of the soul absorbed in the eternal contemplation of God." Some Christians believe that the contemplation of God can be achieved while on earth, but to most people such phrases convey nothing more than a form of deep introspection in which the soul is confronted with a vision of boundless light and permeated by a feeling of infinite love. But how is this condition attained? Most Christian mystics agree that its intense forms arise spontaneously, at rare intervals and without any apparent cause.

Eastern religions have this condition of the soul as their very center and raison d'être, although they do not describe it in quite the same terms as do the Christian mystics. For them it is not just an unusual phenomenon which happens to occur among some strangely gifted people called mystics; it is the very life-blood of religion, and comes before doctrines, ethics, or any other aspect of the religious life. The avowed object of Vedanta, Buddhism, and Taoism alike is that man, while living on this earth, may attain a state of mind which is indicated as the understanding of his eternal union and identity with the "Self of the universe." This is the object of Christianity also, but it is not stressed, its psychology is inadequately studied and the many possible ways to its attainment are only vaguely described. In the ordinary way the aim of Christianity is to make the person of Jesus as described in the Gospels as vivid a reality as possible so that the believer may love, follow, and serve Him as if He were a real friend standing always at his side. The psychology of Christian faith is therefore one of the personal devotion of the disciple to his Lord and Master, and this expands into mysticism when the believer feels a relation of love to the cosmic as well as to the personal Christ. In the ordinary way it is impossible to separate the psychology of Christian religion from a specific personality and specific beliefs concerning him, and thus it is not always easy for the Christian to recognize that a similar, if not identical, state of soul can be attained by one who has never heard of Jesus of Nazareth.

This in no way invalidates the Christian experience. It only means that in Christianity there is no clear division between the psychology of spiritual experience and religious doctrine and history. The Christian belief that only one historical religious tradition is valid for man is a clear enough sign of this confusion; so much emphasis is placed on history and doctrine as the essentials of salvation that a psychology of religion independent of the person of Christ is not understood. In the three great Eastern religions this confusion does not exist, and from them we are able to form a much clearer idea of the essentials of religion, of the state of mind called spiritual experience as distinct from the "local color" of particular historical events. For if indeed this experience is attainable outside the Christian faith, apart from devotion to a particular personality, and even without reference to theology (as in certain forms of Buddhism), then Eastern religions have two important contributions to make to Western civilization. Firstly, they show the principles of an approach to spiritual experience on a purely psychological basis to those who have lost faith in the historical and theological tenets of Christianity; secondly, Christianity itself can be enriched and expanded in this sadly underdeveloped aspect of its experience, and perhaps led to a higher understanding of spirituality than even many of its own mystics have attained.[9]

EASTERN WISDOM AND MODERN MAN

The wisdom of the East is something from which we can *learn* but which we should be careful not to *imitate*. It is unwise for a Westerner to become "converted" to Buddhism or Hinduism as missionaries expect the "heathen" to become converted to Christianity, for there are aspects of the Eastern religions which would be decidedly harmful for us to adopt. We cannot escape our roots and traditions, which are different from those of Asiatic peoples, for we have a different function or *dharma* to fulfill in the world. We have already said that acceptance is not necessarily a matter of mental or physical passivity, but we find a certain kind of passivity insisted upon in all the great religions of the East, for the Asiatic attitude to life has a decided element of quietism and laissez faire—an attitude which is encouraged by their religious technique. For them this attitude is right, but European and American psychology is active and assertive and it would not be right for us to deny this active urge. Therefore it is important for us in our study of Oriental religion to distinguish between principles and their application; the principles have universal value, but, generally speaking, their application has been worked out to accord only with Asiatic peoples and conditions. We have to discover our own way of applying those principles, and though *in the end* this may lead us to something like Oriental passivity it would be the greatest mistake to begin by imitating it.

The outward forms of this passivity are seen in yoga meditation, a pacifism (*ahimsa*) extended even to animals, a total disregard for material progress and social service, and a lofty detachment from material concerns in general. It is often that in the applied philosophy of the East the world of form and action is illusion (*maya*) and does not merit the wise man's attention; but this is *applied* philosophy and not a fundamental principle, according to which the universe cannot be absolutely divided into illusion and reality, seeing that the ultimate is non-dual and includes all opposites. It is impossible for anyone not inured to it by tradition to regard the world as illusion by a mere decision of the will, for imitation of other people's ideas is as false as imitation of their behavior. But Oriental introversion and Occidental extraversion are alike essential and equally important human functions, the one without the other being as sterile as man without woman. To grasp the essentials of Oriental wisdom we do not have to imitate its externals; it is neither necessary nor wise, as some theosophists and would-be Buddhists and yogis imagine, for us to go and sit at the feet of masters in India or Tibet, to assume the life of the homeless *sanyassin*, and to adopt the technique of Eastern meditation in order to attain spiritual freedom. Having attained that freedom, however, there is no reason why one should not study Eastern meditation as much as one pleases if one happens to be interested in it. But to look for actual salvation, happiness, or enlightenment in it is asking for trouble because it is almost impossible to avoid both imitation in itself and imitation of something that belongs to an alien tradition.[10]

THE DANGER OF THE INFLATED EGO

Anyone who has studied either Hinduism, Buddhism, or Taoism will know that the object of these religions is to attain a realization of the union between man and the Self of the universe. In their scriptures they describe various psychological techniques by which this may be achieved, and many Western people who approach them from a practical standpoint simply follow the directions as given. The result is not very happy. Such people do not appreciate the vast difference between the psychology of modern man and the psychology of the ancient Chinese or Hindus. Their scriptures state very plainly that the true Self of man is God. *Tat tvam asi* is the Hindu formula, meaning, "That (Brahman or God) art thou." This is also the theme of several forms of Western mysticism; in the words of Eckhart, "While I am here, He is in me; after this life, I am in Him. All things are therefore possible to me, if I am united to Him Who can do all things." And again, "I have a capacity in my soul for taking in God entirely. I am sure as I live that nothing is so near to me as God. God is nearer to me than I am to myself; my existence depends on the nearness and presence of God. He is also near things of wood and stone, but they know it not. If a piece of wood became as aware of the nearness of God as an archangel is, the piece of wood would be as happy as an archangel."[11] But for the modern Westerner there is a danger in this knowledge; reading and practicing such ideas he is apt to make a God of his ego rather than an ego of his God.

Until modern man has truly understood the meaning of his apparent divorce from nature, his acute sense of separateness and self-consciousness, he cannot possibly understand the teaching that his true Self is God. If he makes any attempt to impose this teaching upon himself, he is more than likely to suffer a spiritual inflation, a blowing-up of his ego to the size of God, which is the very thing that Oriental philosophy does *not* desire. This happens because the unfortunate victim has not first accepted the division and the conflict. He has not allowed God to be an ego; he has denied the purpose of nature in evolving the sense of separateness, and until he has accepted it all his attempts to resolve the problem will be in terms of egoism. In other words, unless you accept all that the loneliness and isolation of self-consciousness involves every attempt to get away from it will be futile. The ego cannot abolish the pain of conflict between itself and the universe simply by trying to identify itself with the essence of that universe which is God. Paradoxically, it must realize its union with God by *being an ego*, for the very reason that *that is what God Himself is doing* in that particular human being. In fact modern man's path to this wisdom is roundabout and not direct, and he must always bear in mind the saying, "Before you can unite, you must first divide."

THE IMPORTANCE OF GODS AND DEMONS

There is still another reason why the wisdom of the East cannot be imitated. It has to be understood against the background of popular belief among Asiatic peoples. The wisdom of the East was taught among men who firmly believed in the existence of innumerable gods, demons, elemental spirits, and angels, who were familiar with all the potentialities of the human soul both for good and for evil, and whose personal and social lives were hardly regulated, even in theory, by what we should call reason. We, on the other hand, do not have anything to do with gods and demons; we do not believe that men's souls can be possessed by autonomous devils except in certain cases of lunacy, to which we give the relatively harmless name of "obsession." We think we are masters of our minds (or should be) and that such beliefs are outworn superstitions. In the universe of science everything happens for a reason and no room is left for the gods to interfere.

What is the result? Simply that the demons, having been driven out of the external universe, return with a vengeance in our own souls and behave quite as irrationally. For in proving to ourselves that the universe is wholly explainable in terms of reason and logic, we ourselves become anything but reasonable and logical. We starve in the midst of unparalleled abundance and wage diabolical wars when everybody knows that nothing can be gained from war, when for years everyone has (consciously) been trying to avoid war—yes, even those who thought they could "get away with murder" without starting a war. Of course, the old-fashioned psychologist could give a perfectly logical and reasoned explanation of human irrationality, but we are not speaking in those terms. We are looking at the situation from a purely empirical standpoint and noting that the more men try to dominate life by conscious reason, the more irrational they become. We are not saying for a moment that the logical explanation of the universe given by science is untrue; we are simply noting with interest that such an explanation and such an age exist together, that in a time when science is unusually logical, men are unusually stupid. We are therefore entitled to assume a connection between these two phenomena, for the psychologist is not interested in the truth or untruth of scientific theories; he wants to know *why* those theories are acceptable to modern man. He is also rude enough to suggest that people believe in them not because the theories or the people are logical, but because the people want to be logical.

In other words, the reasons for belief in a logical universe would have to be invented if they were not true. As Bernard Shaw says, belief is a matter of taste and is quite unaffected by the objective truth or falsity of that belief. Our belief in a logical universe is a matter of taste, even though it may be objectively true; we say we are reasonable men, but we accept the pronouncements of our scientists with a faith quite as groveling as the faith of peasants who believe unquestioningly those who say they have seen gods and demons. How many people could prove such common beliefs as that the earth revolves round the sun or that atoms are composed of electrons and protons?

But who are the gods and demons whom we have tried to cast out of our lives? They are the forces of that unknown, inner universe of the unconscious, though to-day we give them the unromantic names of impulses, depressions, phobias, manias, and other constant reminders of the fact that our inner lives are not so much under our control or even under our surveillance as we should like to think. These forces are projected by other races than our own into deific and demonic forms which play an important part in everyday life, and those who were instructed in many of the ancient religions had to recognize the existence of those beings within themselves. But we are slow in recognizing them at all, much less in ourselves, and from that point of view we are in a worse psychological position even than the "heathen Chinese" who really believes in their external existence. For whether or not the "heathen Chinese" is aware of their true nature, he is nevertheless aware of irrational forces at work in his life, and even that much awareness gives him a certain release from them. Naturally there is a considerable difference in Asiatic lands between religion for serious students and religion for the masses, but in the former the gods and demons are still preserved though there is a difference of understanding. Western students of Oriental religion should never neglect the study of its iconography, especially in Hinduism and Buddhism, for there it will be found that almost every god, Buddha, and Bodhisattva has his demonic counterpart. The student may be surprised to find, however, that these demonic counterparts are not regarded as evil in our sense of the word although the forms in which they are painted and carved are diabolic in the extreme.

I have before me a Japanese painting of the Buddhist divinity Nilambara-Vajrapani which might easily be a portrait of that monster the Dweller on the Threshold of Western mysticism.[12] His body is black and he wears a tigerskin adorned with skulls; he has some eighteen heads wreathed with serpents, and upon each are three glaring eyes above snarling lips and bared teeth; serpents coil around each of his twenty-eight arms and in his hands he grasps swords and thunderbolts while other monsters grovel beneath his feet. Behind the whole figure is an aureole of writhing vermilion flame. In all his outward aspects he might be taken for an Oriental version of Satan himself, until one discovers that he is one of the *guardians* of the Law of Buddhism. Going to even more ancient sources one discovers the same idea, for Iamblichos, writing on the Egyptian Mysteries, says:[13]

> The race of demons . . . causes the otherwise invisible goodness of the gods to become visible in operation, becoming itself both assimilated to it, and accomplishing perfect works that are like it. For then what was before unutterable in it is made capable of being uttered.

We, too, have a popular but perhaps neglected saying that God created the Devil for those who could not learn by love, and it cannot be by mere chance that his name is Lucifer, the light-bearer. But somehow the demons became identified with evil, and this seems to have been part of the necessary but repressive mission of Christianity. Christianity made the demonic light-bearer evil, but our modern age does not even allow the demons to be evil; it does not allow them to exist at all, and it is noticeable that in most forms of modernistic Christianity the subject of the Devil is either tactfully avoided or explained away.

THE CONSCIOUS RELATIONSHIP

From this it seems that before we can approach Oriental wisdom in any way resembling the Asiatic approach we must first become conscious again of the various demonic powers which our civilization has relegated to the unconscious. Furthermore, we shall have to learn the actual *beneficence* of those powers. They represent the dark side of life, being the earthy aspects of divine activity—the deep urges of the physical body, the storms of emotion, the principle of death and destruction, and all those irrational passions that the cult of reason will not tolerate. This is not to be confused, however, with such modern phenomena as Nazi psychology with its cult of blood and soil. Such cults are rationalization and logic run wild and denote possession by those powers, not in any sense a conscious relationship with them, for Nazi philosophy also includes the complete rationalization and regimentation of social and personal life—a very suggestive combination, and a warning.

Thus at the present time modern man is unconsciously identified with his gods and demons, and while they remain unknown he cannot arrive at any conscious relationship to them; he cannot accept his "inner universe" until he knows what kind of things he has to accept, until he can see it objectively and break up the identification. In this present state the blind adoption of Oriental mysticism would simply perpetuate and aggravate his condition; in trying to identify himself with God he would become more and more possessed by the unconscious powers of his inner universe. This is not what Oriental mysticism means by "identification" with God, which is not unconscious possession but the result of fulfilling a conscious relationship between the ego and its inner and outer universes. In twentieth-century civilization such a relationship is rare indeed.

Union through conscious relationship is illustrated in the accompanying diagram. The first circle represents the primitive, unconsciously *lived* by Nature, and with only a limited self-consciousness. The second represents modern, Western man, still unconsciously driven yet at the same time aware of the difference between himself and the natural, external universe. If he flees from that opposition along the line marked "escape" he simply continues to be driven and so possessed by unconscious forces. The third represents the principle of conscious union, of approaching God or Nature through accepting the difference between that and one's own ego—or more correctly by accepting

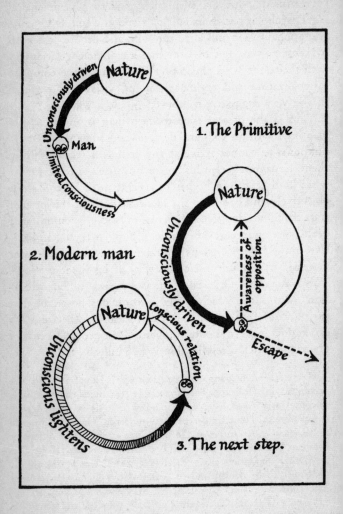

1. The Primitive

Nature

Man

Unconsciously driven

Limited consciousness

2. Modern man

Nature

Unconsciously driven

Awareness of opposition

Escape

3. The next step.

Nature

Conscious relation

Unconscious lightens

the tension caused by an apparent difference. The full union described in Oriental philosophy would be represented by a continuation of the third circle to the point where man coincides with Nature; this would be the same symbol as the familiar Oriental motif of the serpent biting its tail. Note that the first two are not complete circles; the circle is only completed when the opposition is accepted, and this completion is a symbol of the feeling of harmony in the midst of opposition.

PSYCHOLOGY VERSUS METAPHYSICS

If this problem has to be approached in the way described above, it will be asked whether Oriental philosophy has any value at all for us at the present time. We have already drawn attention to a certain "trickiness" in the problem of acceptance; it is precisely in dealing with this that the East is of value to us. We must learn, however, to concentrate on the *psychology* of Oriental religion as distinct from its *metaphysics*. In fact, it is very doubtful whether its metaphysics was ever intended to be taken as metaphysics. For Oriental philosophy is emphatically not philosophy in the Western sense of the word, having scarcely any relation to the intellectual search for objective, metaphysical truth which we find in Descartes, Berkeley, Hegel, and other Western metaphysicians.

Thus the Oriental doctrine of the union of man and Brahman is the symbol of a psychological experience rather than a statement of objective fact, and it is almost impossible to study Oriental religion with profit unless one is always careful to inquire into the experience behind the doctrine. But of all the psychological techniques in Oriental religion the most important is that of acceptance (in Chinese *wu-wei*)—a technique which may be applied in a number of different directions. It is not for us to apply it exactly in their way; our method, as we have seen, has to be somewhat indirect, for we have to apply this technique to the opposition between ego and universe. Yet in so doing we shall arrive at the same result, though by a different route, and discover that *wu-wei* is more than technique; it is an actual spiritual experience, absolutely independent of metaphysics. Thus for the Oriental and Westerner both the experience and the technique are the same, but the approach, the direction in which the technique is applied, differs in each instance. Generally speaking, I would say that whereas the former accepts the universe, the latter must accept the ego and the conflict involved. But, as has been shown, this amounts *in the end* to the same thing because it will eventually be realized that the ego and its conflict are necessary aspects of universal life, of the Tao, Brahman, God, or whatever the ultimate reality may be called.

One exception must be made to this statement. It is important to remember Jung's warning that there are still among us people whose sense of self-consciousness is not yet fully developed, who still share the primitive's *participation mystique* with nature. They are easily overwhelmed by unconscious forces, as in obsessions, and sometimes find it hard to distinguish between fantasy and real life. Such people must first experience the independence of the ego; otherwise they will find themselves hopelessly overwhelmed in any attempt to deal with their "gods and demons" by acceptance.[14]

In conclusion we may say that for Western man acceptance means this: "Live and let live." We see the root of our unhappiness in the war between ourselves and the universe, a war in which we so often feel tiny, impotent, and alone.

The forces of nature, death, change, and unreasoning passion, seem to be against our most cherished longings, and by no trick or deceit can we get rid of our helpless solitude or of the battle between desire and destiny. Acceptance for us is therefore to say, "Let it live" to the whole situation, to the ego and its desires, to life and destiny, and also to the war between them. This acceptance is made in the knowledge that the conflict and all its parties are aspects of a single living activity which employs a seeming discord to achieve the understanding of a harmony which in fact has never been and never can be broken. This is to fulfill the purpose of that conflict, a purpose which is denied when the ego strives to arrogate to itself identity with God—an identity achieved simply in being an ego and in being true to its self-conscious nature. This, however, cannot possibly be understood in any deep sense until the situation as it is now has been accepted, whereat it will develop in its own natural course into a new and different situation. But it is also necessary to understand the conflict, to become aware of its existence and character not only in external circumstances but also in the soul of man, and of the latter we are very ignorant. Therefore it seems wise to consult the wisdom of the East both in accepting and in understanding, in finding an appropriate way of life which, for reasons that will be apparent, psychology alone does not as yet supply.

Those powers of the human soul which the ancients called gods and demons are not deprived of their magic by changing their names. For they retain the same godlike and demonic characteristics, even though in fact they may not wear halos and wings or horns and spiked tails. In calling them gods and demons the ancients may have been fanciful, but at least they were aware of an important fact which we too often overlook, namely, that those powers have a life of their own which is altogether independent of our conscious desire and will. This is what we are so apt to forget when trying to deal with our moods—when, for instance, a powerful depression lays hold on us or when we are seized with a sudden, violent hatred. Such phenomena are not peculiar to individuals; whole nations or continents may be possessed in the same way, and a people may be led into war or other forms of political madness despite the strongest protests of conscious reason. Nowadays we say that such people have lost their self-control; the ancients would have said that they were possessed by devils, and between those two diagnoses there is all the difference in the world. For the former implies no more than a mere failure of conscious will, whereas the latter recognizes that many more factors than conscious will have to be taken into account in the ordering of human life.

THE LANGUAGE OF THE UNCONSCIOUS

But, as we have already seen, there is a tendency among us to recognize our gods and demons again, a tendency represented by the growing popularity of the psychology of the unconscious. This new science has not only revealed the unconscious origin of such familiar states of mind as moods and phobias; it has also revealed gods and demons almost totally lost to consciousness, as for instance the Freudian Œdipus Complex and even more remote powers described by Jung as the *anima*, the *animus*, the Shadow, the Terrible Mother, the Wise Old Man and the Mana-Personality.[1] Their very names call to mind the myths and legends of the ancient world. These "unconscious contents" are various aspects of what we have described as man's unknown, inner universe, and the aim of psychological science is to bring them to consciousness in order that we may define a conscious relationship to them instead of being their unwitting instruments. This science originally came into being to assist in the cure of psychotic and neurotic conditions, but subsequently many of its followers have seen in it the possibilities of greater development of personality for so-called "normal" people as well. In cases of lunacy and psychosis we see the conscious ego completely overwhelmed by forces that enter but slightly or not at all into normal consciousness. At any moment a sudden shock may sweep the ego off its feet and leave any one of us a prey to mental mechanisms which in the ordinary way the ego keeps in their place. For it seems as if the ego were the organizing faculty whose function is to "make sense" out of a collection of chaotic powers. But when it is unaware of those powers it is liable at any time to surreptitious invasion or even to "open aggression," and at the same time there is always the dim awareness of conflict between ourselves and our demons. This awareness becomes more acute when we are in the throes of a mood, but for the sake of comfort we usually do our best to banish the sense of conflict and to forget that our souls contain subversive elements which must constantly be kept in order.

But all attempts to ignore the internal conflict lead us into trouble. This may be clarified by a simple illustration, typical of many cases that come to the psychologist's attention. A man finds himself unaccountably unhappy in his marriage and goes to a psychologist for advice. The psychologist asks him many questions about the situation, and discovers that the man is upset because there is a mysterious "something" which his wife fails to give him. Stimulated by discussing the problem with another person, he dreams the following night that he comes home from his office to find that his wife is out. He thinks he will take a bath while waiting for her to come back for dinner, but on going to the bathroom he finds the tub already filled with dirty, soapy water. He is just about to pull out the stopper when an octopus emerges and wraps its tentacles around his wrist. He wakes in terror. Questioned by the psychologist he remarks that his wife is often in the habit of taking a bath at the time he returns from work. Instead of her he finds the octopus, but does that mean that his marriage is unhappy because his wife is a vampire, is just out for his money and will discard him when she has sucked him dry? On the contrary, the symbols of the unconscious which we meet in dreams refer to one's own attitude to the situation, and in any case the man does not feel this to be at all true of his wife. The psychologist then asks him about his attitude to his mother, and discovers that he was very much attached to her and moreover that she was in the habit of protecting him as much as possible from responsibility—a protection which he secretly enjoyed. In fact, with his own connivance, his mother did not allow him to live his own life. Thereupon the psychologist suggests that the octopus represents his mother who virtually sucked away his manly virility, his capacity to face the world on his own feet. But why does he find the octopus where he would ordinarily find his wife? Perhaps this gives a clue to the mysterious "something" which he finds lacking in her, which he desires so much and the absence of which is making his marriage unhappy. Indeed it does, for the trouble is that his wife will not mother him and relieve him of responsibilities. He married her under the unconscious delusion that she would take the place of his mother, and the dream shows him his desire to return to maternal protection in the form of an octopus.

Now the octopus, the spider, and the crab are familiar symbols for the "Terrible Mother," which is the name given to an irrational desire to regress to an infantile condition, to return to the protected irresponsibility of the infant or to the comfortable, sleepy darkness of the womb. The desire appears under these terrible symbols because, from the conscious standpoint, it is a demon which denies the power of the ego and the rational ideal of progress to greater and greater heights of independence and self-direction. Thus there is always a conflict between the ego and this regressive desire, this principle of inertia and backsliding which the Hindus called *tamas*. If that conflict is repressed and left unrecognized, the desire tricks the ego into situations where the conflict will be continued and intensified in various disguises. Thus, in the above case, the conflict between husband

and wife was the continuation of an unresolved conflict between the husband and his desire to slip back to infantile irresponsibility, to the protection of the mother.

NEUROSIS AND GENIUS

That very desire may often lie behind religious feeling when people seek a substitute for the mother in God or in the *Mother* Church, but it would be absurd to suggest that such desires are the raison d'être of religion. The suggestion is rather that genuine religion is difficult to achieve until these conflicts have been recognized, for religion becomes too easily an escape from the awareness of the war in the soul. This is why it is most important for us to be careful when our culture is being invaded by new and captivating religious forms from the Orient. If we are to make proper use of those forms it is essential that we use them for their correct purpose—to resolve the conflict, not to hide it—and this is more important than ever in an age which is particularly blind to its gods and demons.

But now as to practical ways and means, *how* is this recognition of the inner conflict to be achieved, and how is it to be resolved? Should we turn from priest and philosopher to doctor and psychologist, should we watch our dreams and fantasies, learn the meaning of their symbols and become intimately acquainted with the unconscious universe? In the present state of psychological practice I would hesitate very much to advise any great reliance upon its technique except in cases of a specific psychological difficulty or an insupportable neurosis. In dealing with such matters it is of the greatest use, but beyond this its technique is at present somewhat inadequate and unless supported by other factors, such as religion, might well do more harm than good. In any case, no competent psychologist will allow his patient to "indulge" in analysis as a substitute for actual life.

From one point of view it is true that almost everyone suffers from some form of neurosis, however mild, but the cure of neurosis by itself is not generally desirable unless one of two other conditions is involved: first, that the neurosis is unbearable, and second, that the psychology can supply a source of creative energy to take the place of the neurosis. In fact, we have neurosis to thank for some of the greatest human genius, for the very motive of escape from conflict has provided a driving force for artistic and scientific accomplishments very worth while in themselves, and possession by unconscious forces is the secret of many a creative genius. It may indeed be possible to attribute the masterpieces of Leonardo da Vinci[2] to unresolved problems of infantile sexuality, and maybe the sonnets of Shakespeare were the work of a homosexual pervert. It is also possible that if they had been psychoanalyzed their names would never have been remembered, and some of us would prefer all manner of secret perversions to cultural and spiritual impotence. Almost everyone can number among his friends people who have achieved greatness out of an "inferiority complex" or repressed sexuality; such greatness is not invariably beneficial, but who would see the world deprived of its great saints and its great sinners just for the sake of "normality"? It is true, of course, that in later years many of the world's geniuses have been overtaken and ruined by the conflict they struggled so hard to escape; yet it should be remembered that we pay for the beauty of the rose with the rottenness of the manure. It is the old story of the pairs of opposites.

JUNG'S ANALYTICAL PSYCHOLOGY

But, on the other hand, there have lived men of genius who in some way resolved this opposition, whose creative power had no roots in neurosis. Can the psychology of the unconscious reveal their secret? Does it offer any source of energy to take the place of the neurosis it cures? So far the most serious attempt to tackle this problem is the work of Jung. Others, partly allied to his school and partly independent, have contributed—notably Heyer and Prinzhorn in Germany, Assagioli in Italy, Hadfield, Graham Howe, and the Pastoral Psychologists in England, and Beatrice Hinkle in America.[3] The system of Jung in particular deserves careful attention because it provides an important link with the psychology of the Orient. Generally speaking, we may say that his system of analytical psychology falls into two departments which, to some extent, overlap. One is the cure of neurosis and the other the re-creation of the individual. In many cases the one follows the other, so that a Jungian analysis is more than often not just the solution of a particular problem but a radical "overhauling" and remaking of the personality, and I have known cases where the analysis has been carried on for from ten to twenty years. This is not surprising, for radical changes in the spiritual life are not achieved in from ten to twenty months; often it is the work of a lifetime.

There is no hard-and-fast technique for the re-creation of the individual on Jungian lines, but the process usually follows certain general principles.[4] By various means, including attention to dreams and fantasies and discussion with the analyst, the symbols of the unconscious are brought to light and the individual endeavors to discover their meaning for himself and define his attitude to them. These symbols are the forms or "archetypes" under which the gods and demons appear, and as the individual comes to terms with them he brings about certain psychological changes in himself. There appears to be almost a hierarchy of these archetypes, for when one is consciously assimilated another appears, and the situations resulting from this assimilation are represented in key dreams. These key dreams differ from ordinary dreams in their obviously symbolic character, for the figures which appear bear the closest resemblance to archaic religious and mythological forms. Frequently the dreamer witnesses forms and symbols of which he has never had any conscious knowledge, and it is not uncommon for a series of key dreams to bear close resemblance to the stages of ancient initiation rites.

But the process does not consist simply in watching over one's dreams; it is fundamentally a question of the conscious assimilation and acceptance of hitherto unconscious processes, in spite of their seeming irrationality and independence of the ego. When this has been carried out successfully for some time, a fundamental change is said to take place in the psyche. This Jung describes as a shifting of the center of personality from the ego to the self, a term which, in his system, has the special meaning of the center of the whole psyche as distinct from the center of consciousness, which is the ego. He explains the self as a "virtual point" between the conscious and the unconscious which gives equal recognition to the demands of both. Dreams representing this situation usually appear in the form of the *mandala*, the magic circle, the golden flower, the rose at the center of the cross and similar figures representing wholeness, balance, and attainment of a spiritual center.[5]

Individuation

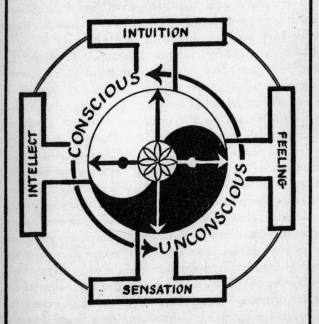

The Wheel on the Cross.

An interesting feature of these *mandala* is that the divisions of the circle or the petals of the flower are usually four or multiples of four. This is explained as a sign of the complete development of the individual in all his four faculties or functions—intuition, sensation, intellect, and feeling. Jung maintains that generally speaking only one, two, or three of these faculties are active; the dormant faculties are "contaminated" by the unconscious, which is to say identified with an archetypal form. (Of course, those who pay no attention to their dreams see no archetypal forms with which their dormant faculties can be identified. For them we may say that the faculty is just undeveloped and so unconscious.) Thus in dreams the inferior faculty is often personified by the *anima* figure in men, which is to say the female image (usually a goddess) in whose form the unconscious is liable to appear and make its pronouncements. In women its place is taken by the *animus*—a male figure.

Naturally the unconscious is an unfamiliar realm and for most people the descriptive language of Jungian psychology is so much mysterious jargon. We read a lot about *animus, anima,* inferior functions, archetypes, *mandala,* key dreams, and so forth, and begin to wonder whether someone is not a little crazy. Of course, to understand these various "denizens of the deep" we have to have personal experience of them, and this is most effectively had in dreams and in the conscious assimilation of dream symbols. For in dreaming the conscious is a little sleepy and incompetent; it is not interfering so efficiently with other mental processes, and, as everyone knows, between sunset and dawn is the ghosts' playtime. But does this mean that before ordinary men and women can achieve any genuine spiritual development they must take careful notes of all their dreams, learn the meaning of their symbols, and even go to an analyst for assistance? I know someone who has been instructed by her analyst to set her alarm clock to ring every hour during the night so that she can wake up and write her dreams in a notebook. Yet it is very easy to be unfair in this matter for the whole technique lends itself to caricature in the hands both of analysts and of hostile satirists. The only important question is not whether the process is a nuisance but whether it works. Does it make possible the re-creation of the individual?

THE MEANING OF INDIVIDUATION

First of all, we must ask what, in plain language as distinct from jargon, it proposes to do. It proposes to adapt the individual to his inner universe, to the unconscious natural urges within himself in such a way that his entire being is made into a total, related organism with a conscious center of gravity and balance. It presupposes that the unconscious, being nature in man, is the source of vitality, and assumes that its creative power can be most effectively handled when the ego provides it with an unobstructed but nevertheless directed channel. Whereas the neurotic genius finds his energy in escape and the natural genius in "possession" by unconscious forces ("which is to madness close allied"), the integrated genius would supposedly be able to draw upon the unconscious life-sources quite freely and consciously. I do not know how this can be expressed more concretely, and I believe this language must remain an utter mystery to those who have no feeling whatever of an unconscious life within themselves. When your life is centered wholly in consciousness it is naturally impossible to understand the meaning of another kind of center. If you were aware only of your head, it would be impossible to have any feeling for your solar plexus.

But there is, perhaps, one other way in which it may be related to ordinary, everyday experience. Many people feel at times that they have more than one soul; this is particularly true of children and primitives. Lafcadio Hearn describes a conversation on this subject with a Japanese peasant who tells him that a man may have as many as nine souls, the number varying in accordance with his spiritual perfection. The more souls the better, but it is important that however many souls you may be given you should keep them together. "Sometimes," he says, "they may be separated. But if the souls of a man be separated, that man becomes mad. Mad people are those who have lost one of their souls."[6] This feeling of a multiplicity of souls seems to be a rudimentary awareness of the unconscious and more especially of the independent character of its forces. Children feel changes in their personality from day to day; in many cases one finds, for instance, the most remarkable changes in their handwriting, and it is marvelous to see how sincerely they can play at being other people and things. But as adults we are apt to forget our many souls, and in passing from adolescence to adulthood become more settled and centered in our mental behavior. I think the re-creation of the personality might fairly be described as becoming conscious again of our plurality, of our many souls, and having them all contribute to our being instead of one at a time. "Genius," said Novalis, "is perhaps nothing more than the result of inward Plurality." One is reminded, too, of the words of Shakespeare's Richard II:

My brain I'll prove the female to my soul,
My soul the father: and these two beget
A generation of still-breeding thoughts,
And these same thoughts people this little world,
In humors like the people of this world,
For no thought is contented. The better sort,—
As thoughts of things divine,—are intermixed
With scruples, and do set the word itself
Against the word.

THE DANGER OF BEWITCHMENT

But now we are left with the question: does this method
of analytical psychology work? Have the symbols of spiritual attainment which may be experienced in dreams any
relation to actual fact, to the individual's deepest responses
to life—in short, to his happiness? Actually this is not
quite a fair question, because it is never just to judge a
system by all the people who follow it. I have no doubt
at all that it works, *with the right people*. The Chinese
have a saying that "when the wrong man uses the right
means, the right means work in the wrong way."[7] Jung
himself is the first to admit the truth of this saying, for, in
his own words, "when it comes to things like these, everything depends on the man and little or nothing on the
method." But the system of analytical psychology does not
always seem to attract the right people, and this is often true
of those who go into it with a view to becoming analysts.

Fortunately, however, there are those in Jung's school
who are keenly aware of this danger, and it is well that they
should watch it, not only for their own sake, but also because similar difficulties lie in the path of every other ven-
ture into the unconscious mind, and for that matter in the
path of every human being who seeks adaptation to his

inner universe. Jung has gone far more deeply into the nature of the unconscious than did Freud,[8] and his system is bound up with aspects of the human soul which have a peculiar magic. Indeed, he goes so deeply that to follow him, not in ideas alone but in experience, is an extremely serious undertaking which involves the gravest risks for those whose feet are not planted on solid earth. And here "fools rush in where angels fear to tread." The deeper images and forces of the unconscious have a fascination, an irresistible glamour which casts a spell on those who are not, as we say, "plain tough." I believe Jung himself to be very conscious of this danger, and were he a less competent man his work might have the most unfortunate results. For he is open to the same dangers of personal adulation and misuse of his discoveries that threaten the work of all great leaders in spiritual adventure. These dangers are somewhat intensified by the nature of analytical work, but nothing worth while was ever achieved without risk. As long as he and his immediate colleagues continue to insist, as they do, that analysis is no substitute for actual living, and that it certainly must not be indulged in for the sake of its powerful glamour, they will be doing all in their power to rid the system of its abuses. Every system, whether of psychology or religion, has its abusers, but analytical psychology contains particularly strong dynamite which it will always do well to guard.

There are those who go a long way in the re-creative work of analytical psychology and yet have all spoiled by their inability to shake off the spell of the unconscious and its mystical figures. When this happens the process defeats its own purpose. It is intended to make the individual a free, genuine person in his own right; but under the spell he becomes utterly dependent on the system as such, goes in for the study of psychology in a big way and generally wallows around in its captivating atmosphere. Certainly it provides glamour and mystery which seem rather lacking in the stark realities of ordinary life, but when the system becomes an end instead of a means it is a millstone about one's neck instead of a liberator. At this point the analyst has to bring his patient back to earth with a bump. This fascination is a danger constantly besetting the professional teacher or practitioner of religion or psychology. The study of the unconscious for its own sake is only safe for those who can forget the subject completely without feeling that they are suffering any loss. A Chinese allegory of the spiritual life known as the Ten Oxherding Pictures represents the use of religion in the form of catching and herding an ox.[9] But when the herdsman has caught it and ridden home on its back, he does not take it into his house with him; he puts it away and forgets it. The commentary to the picture reads: "When you know that what you need is not the snare or set-net but the hare or fish, it is like gold separated from the dross, it is like the moon rising out of the clouds." The system, which carries you on its back for a while, is the ox, but if you can't get rid of it you would have done better never to have gone after it, unless, of course, you are compelled to accept this thraldom as the lesser of two evils. Unfortunately the mysteries of analytical psychology so captivate certain types of people that they mistake such bewitchment for the feeling of a vocation to be a psychologist.

As now practiced, psychology is no more a way of life than medicine and surgery. Physicians and surgeons have to know the structure of the body down to the last detail, but it is not necessary to have that knowledge to lead a healthy physical life. In the same way, the practicing psychologist has to know the psyche just as thoroughly; it does not follow that the same intimate knowledge is necessary for mental health. No sensible doctor who is not a shark advises the removal of a patient's appendix, tonsils, adenoids, teeth, ovaries, and anything else that may occur to him just in case they might give trouble. Only a faddist goes to his doctor every day to discuss his insides and make sure that he is living in accordance with the rules of health. Nevertheless, both the doctor and the psychologist are in a position to make certain observations about healthy living, to lay down certain principles which do not involve constant preoccupation with the more intimate details of the internal organs. Therefore it seems most unwise to make any *deliberate* attempt to bring the deeper contents of the unconscious to light, unless for strictly scientific and professional reasons—which are not the same as spiritual reasons. For one's degree of spirituality does not depend on *how much* of your unconscious you have assimilated; it depends on how ready you are to accept and assimilate it when it comes in its own time. Which is another way of repeating that knowledge and experience are not to be confused with wisdom.

THE AIMS OF PSYCHOTHERAPY

This is where the psychology of the West can take a lesson from the psychology of the East, which pays more attention to the way of acceptance and less to the things to be accepted. It is interested in creating a state of mind that will be prepared for all eventualities, all surprises both from the outer and from the inner universes. It does not go out of its way, looking for things to accept. Far too little emphasis is laid on this aspect of the work by ill-advised practitioners of the psychology of the unconscious, and as a result analysis can easily have a certain remoteness from life. Analysis is not something on which one can work only at night, in dreamland, and psychological health cannot be bought at ten dollars a visit every Thursday afternoon. A friend who called on me one evening suddenly announced that he had to go home early because his analyst had instructed him to "face a problem." When the facing of problems and the acceptance of life is too studied, when it requires that you go home early, shut yourself in your room and solemnly sit down, take the problem out of a drawer and *face* it, we begin to wonder what has become of a certain indispensable quality called humor. Analysis is not intended to be remote from life at all, but when overmuch emphasis is laid on the dream, on unconscious symbolism, unconscious drawing and painting, and on the life of fantasy in general there is a danger of dividing life into two halves and neglecting the relations between them, as if the whole process required nothing more than development in the dream and fantasy world.

Many of these difficulties would be overcome by a clear understanding of the aims of psychological work by those who are unable to avail themselves of a wise analyst, and here again the view of such Oriental systems as Taoism and various forms of Buddhism is very suggestive. For here the object is not to reach any particular *stage*; it is to find the right attitude of mind in whatever stage one may happen to be. This, indeed, is a fundamental principle of those forms of Oriental psychology which we shall be considering. In the course of his evolution man will pass through an indefinite number of stages; he will climb to the crest of one hill to find his road leading on over the crest of another and another. No stage is final because the meaning of life is in its movement and not in the place to which it moves. We have a proverb that to travel well is better than to arrive, which comes close to the Oriental idea. Wisdom does not consist in arriving at a particular place, and no one need imagine that it is necessarily obtained by climbing a ladder whose rungs are the successive stages of psychological experience. That ladder has no end, and the entrance to enlightenment, wisdom, or spiritual freedom may be found on any one of its rungs. If you discover it, it does not mean that you will not have to go on climbing the ladder; you must go on climbing just as you must go on living. But enlightenment is found by accepting fully the place where you stand *now*. Modern man finds himself in the stage of human evolution where there is a maximum division between his ego and the universe; for him, enlightenment is the complete acceptance of that division. Psychological techniques may fail because people do not accept fully the various stages involved; they accept them with the sole object of reaching a certain goal, as for instance the state of "individuation" symbolized by the *mandala*. In such circumstances they may indeed reach that state, but without finding what they inwardly desire. As a result, some people who imagine that they have completed that phase of psychological work are often as unhappy as ever.[10]

Mere exploration of the unconscious is no road to wisdom, for a fool may learn much and experience much but still be a fool. He becomes wise only when he has the humility to let himself be free to be a fool. As Chuang Tzu says, "He who knows he is a fool is not a great fool." For the fool always gives himself away by his pride, by the delusion that greatness is to be measured by mere psychological bulk, and that by loading himself with new experiences he will become a sage. The psychology of the unconscious is his happy hunting ground. "After some five years of analysis," he thinks, "if I work very hard and go through all the necessary stages, I shall become a real person, a genuine, free man." Indeed, that five years' work (the attainment of which will necessitate fooling the analyst too) may teach him something if it happens to show him that he is like the dunce who looked for fire with a lighted lantern. Sometimes the longest way round is the shortest way home.

The way of acceptance and spiritual freedom is found not *by* going somewhere but *in* going, and the stage where its happiness can be known is now, at this very moment, at the very place where you happen to stand. It is in accepting fully your state of soul as it is now, not in trying to force yourself into some other state of soul which, out of pride, you imagine to be a superior and more advanced state. It is not a question of whether your present state is good or bad, neurotic or normal, elementary or advanced; it is a question of what it is. The point is not to accept it *in order* that you may pass on to a "higher" state, but to accept because acceptance in itself *is* that "higher" state, if such it may be called. By way of illustration, here is the story of how the Buddhist sage Hui-neng enlightened Chen Wei-ming who had chased him in order to steal the robe and begging-bowl of the Buddha. Hui-neng had put them both down on a rock, and when Chen tried to lift them he found that they were immovable. At once Chen was terrified, and protested that he had not come for the robe and bowl, but for the wisdom they represented. "Since the object of your coming is for the Dharma," said Hui-neng, "think not of good, think not of evil, but see what your true nature (lit. 'original face') is at this moment." At this Chen was suddenly enlightened; breaking out into a sweat and saluting Hui-neng with tears of joy he asked, "Besides these secret words and hidden meanings which you have just given me, is there anything else which is secret?" Hui-neng replied, "In what I have shown you there is nothing secret. If you reflect and recognize your own true nature, the secret is within you."[11]

PRACTICAL ESSENTIALS

At this time in human history the unconscious becomes a problem because the conflict between nature and the ego is at its height. But this does not mean that for modern man a *full* exploration of the unconscious is necessary for spiritual freedom. This freedom is attainable now, but the unveiling of the unconscious as a special undertaking is a matter of our future evolution and at the present time I do not feel that it should be taken up seriously until the second half of life—a point upon which Jung himself lays particular emphasis.[12] It appears that at the middle of life certain people are ready to undertake a task which *in terms of evolution* will take them a stage beyond the present historical development of civilized man. But this is outside our scope, for here we are concerned with the present rather than the future. This is not to say that there can be no freedom of spirit for young people or for those unready to penetrate the deeper strata of the unconscious. Thus we have to bear in mind always the distinction between the attainment of freedom in regard to *present* conditions, and the future evolution of human consciousness and its faculties. Just because the unconscious has become a problem in present conditions, our more superficial gods and demons demand immediate attention if we are to be free. But, especially for those who have not reached the middle of life, any deeper exploration is out of time and is looking for a problem where none exists.

For all practical purposes it seems important to concentrate less on exploring and unveiling the inner universe and more on the working relationship between that universe (as it now presents itself) and the conscious ego. The essentials are that the individual should know that an inner universe exists, that he should have some idea of its general character, and that he should be ready to assimilate and accept it as and when it makes itself felt. Only harm can result in most cases from digging up its contents for the sake of spiritual development. In other words, when your gods and demons present themselves in emotions, moods, and the like, recognize that they are gods and demons, that they have a life of their own and that you cannot just *will* them out of the way with impunity. In ordinary conditions there is no need to make a special search for the powers of the unknown psyche; they will come of their own accord, and they will be enough of a problem then without looking for more. But when they do come they have to be received, for their power over us is proportionate to the power we use against them.

We have mentioned three essentials in understanding and coming to terms with the inner universe: the knowledge of its existence, the understanding of its general character and the capacity to accept it. These must be considered in more detail, and from the practical standpoint. Many people have no feeling at all of an unconscious mind, much less of an inner universe; others believe intellectually in its existence, but have no experience of it. It is important at the start not to have a misleading conception of it; the unconscious has, so far as we know, no definite location and is not strictly speaking a thing. It is rather a process. The internal universe is not actually located inside the human being; it is, as it were, the relationship between impersonal, natural forces and the unconscious processes of the mind. There is probably no real difference between the internal and external universes; it may be more correct to say that the same universe affects us in two different ways—physically and mentally. In both ways we are unconscious of the greater part of these influences. Thus, if we follow the physical body to its origins, we are led to the universe; the same is true when mental processes are traced to their source, and we find that the connection is both historical and immediate. It is historical as mental heredity, and immediate as mental vitality, for all life is ultimately derived from the mysterious, universal energy that vibrates in the electron.

These, however, are metaphysical considerations, and the psychologist must think in terms of experience. Anyone who is at all aware of himself knows at least something of his many souls, of the deep instinctual and emotional urges which to some extent govern his life. It matters not whether we call them mental or physical; these are only words to describe mysteries whose behavior we know but of whose substance we are utterly ignorant. But our deep urges have undoubtedly a power of their own which, in the long run, is beyond conscious control. No one, for instance, can absolutely stifle the sexual instinct, and however much you may wish to economize by doing without food, your whole being will demand to eat by afflicting you with a savage hunger. It is, for instance, quite beyond our power to control the sex of an unborn child; this matter is wholly in the charge of unconscious factors, as are also the digestion of food and the circulation of the blood. In like manner there are aspects of our psychological life which function instinctively and beyond conscious control.

THE TECHNIQUE OF ACCEPTANCE

If you sit still for a while, completely relaxed, and let your thoughts run on, let your mind think of whatever it likes, without interfering, without making suggestions and without raising any kind of obstacle to the free flow of thought, you will soon discover that mental processes have a life of their own. They will call one another to the surface of consciousness by association, and if you raise no barriers, you will soon find yourself thinking all manner of things both fantastic and terrible which you ordinarily keep out of consciousness. Over a period of time this exercise will show you that you have in yourself the potentiality of countless different beings—the animal, the demon, the satyr, the thief, the murderer—so that in time you will be able to feel that no aspect of human life is strange to you— *humani nihil a me alienum puto*. In the ordinary way consciousness is forever interfering with the waters of the mind, which are dark and turbulent, concealing the depths. But when, for a while, you let them take care of themselves the mud settles and with growing clarity you see the foundations of life and all the denizens of the deep. You may see other things as well. "Two men looked into a pond. Said the one: 'I see a quantity of mud, a shoe and an old can.' Said the other: 'I see all these, but I also see the glorious reflection of the sky.' " For the unconscious is not, as some imagine, a mental refuse-pit; it is simply unfettered nature, demonic and divine, painful and pleasant, hideous and lovely, cruel and compassionate, destructive and creative. It is the source of heroism, love, and inspiration as well as of fear, hatred, and crime. Indeed, it is as if we carried inside of us an exact duplicate of the world we see around us, for the world is a mirror of the soul, and the soul a mirror of the world. Therefore when you learn to feel the unconscious you begin to understand not only yourself but others as well, and when you look upon human crime and stupidity, you can say with real feeling, "There but for the Grace of God go I."

Beyond this it is irrelevant and useless to "prove" the existence of the unconscious. It can only be proved by personal experience, and as a mere conception it is almost valueless. The important thing is to have some *feeling*, however rudimentary, of its existence and of its potentialities for good and for evil. And, after all, to say that we have an unconscious is only another way of saying that mentally and physically we are children of nature and that our lives have roots which go beyond our ken. Sometimes it seems quite impossible that there are those who simply cannot grasp it.

There remains now the question of the capacity to accept the unconscious, and this involves three things: firstly, the capacity to accept its "dark" aspect, secondly, the capacity to accept the *independence* of its "gods and demons" from the ego, and thirdly, the capacity to accept the *conflict* between some of those gods and demons and the ego. It need hardly be said that these capacities are not different; they are the same capacity working in three different but related directions. The process is best shown by a concrete illustration. Let us take, for example, a mood of acute depression. Three things may be said of it: firstly, that it is unpleasant in itself, secondly, that it comes without our consent and does not leave at our command, and thirdly, that we have some reaction to it, a reaction of impatience, disgust, of wishing to be rid of it—which is a factor distinct from and in addition to the feeling of depression itself.

We may call this mood a demon out of the unconscious which has "possessed" us. The way of acceptance begins by giving it our attention. Instead of trying to forget about it and repress it we make up our minds to deal with it consciously, almost as man to man. Instead of allowing our servant at the door (the Freudian "censor") to send it away, we invite it to come in and have a cup of tea. Yes, it would perhaps be better to offer it a Scotch-and-soda— and I mean this in all seriousness, because the idea is to encourage it, to invite it to be itself with a vengeance, really to *be* a depression. For this is accepting its independence of the ego, that is, allowing it to behave as it wills, or, as the Chinese say, to follow its own *tao*, because if we do not allow all other things their *tao* we cannot expect to have our own *tao*. In our own language we might say that to be in accord with nature is to allow everything to follow its own nature. As Lieh Tzu remarked, in explaining the secret of his mysterious capacity to ride on the wind, "I allowed my mind to think without restraint of whatever it pleased and my mouth to talk about whatever it pleased." So here, we allow the depression to take whatever course *it* pleases;

instead of denying it, we affirm it. This requires that we feel our way into its very heart and experience it to the full—one might almost call this a "higher masochism"—and though, to all common sense, it seems the most absurd thing to do, it results in the discovery that even the blackest mood has a profound meaning for us and is a blessing in disguise. It was not without reason that the Egyptians called the demons the mediators between gods and men.

If, however, the conflict between the depression and the ego is particularly strong, we have first to deal with another mediatory demon in the shape of the conflict itself, the feeling of impatience, disgust, and wishing to be rid of it. Sometimes the actual depression is too tough a proposition to tackle directly, and so we have to allow the reactionary feeling of disgust to be itself and behave as it pleases. To this we give full rein in the same way, telling it to be as disgusted, impatient, and angry as it likes. This, of course, affords an immense psychological relief. For it means that the conscious ego has divested itself of the unnecessary and impertinent responsibility of thinking it essential to direct and interfere with all that goes on around it. It is this very sense of false responsibility which disturbs its peace of mind. This is particularly noticeable in cases of insomnia in which people are kept awake by such minor irritations as night noises, doors slamming, trains crossing bridges, cars changing gear, and people moving about the house. The sleepless one immediately assumes a responsibility for these noises in his very wish to interfere with them, and the tension of this responsibility keeps him awake. But if he can allow them to go ahead and clamor as much as they like, he will at once feel relieved, relaxed, and ready for sleep. In such matters it is well to follow the example of one of Edward Lear's inimitable creations:

> There was a young lady whose bonnet
> Came untied when the birds sat upon it.
> But she said, "I don't care,
> For the birds of the air
> Are welcome to sit on my bonnet."

A further illustration is found in the record of a conversation between a Chinese Buddhist teacher and his pupil, who asked the figurative question, "It is terribly hot, and how shall we escape the heat?" The teacher replied, "Go right down to the bottom of the furnace." "But in the furnace," persisted the somewhat baffled pupil, "how shall we escape the scorching fire?" "No further pains will harass you," concluded the teacher. A story is told of a lunatic who used to hit himself on the head with a brick. When asked for an explanation of his peculiar behavior, he answered that it was such a pleasant feeling when he stopped. In the same way we might say that the spiritual raison d'être of suffering is the enlightenment that follows from its acceptance. For the way of acceptance is applicable to demons from both worlds, from the unconscious in the form of depressions, phobias, and the like, and from external circumstances in the form of physical pain and irritation. In this sense acceptance is the philosopher's stone that "turneth all to gold"; it means putting our consciousness in the very core of whatever pain falls upon us and allowing that pain to do its worst. As to our reaction to the pain the same principle applies, for we allow the demon that wishes to scream, protest, and swear all freedom to have its way. As often as not it does not need it, for the very act of granting it the freedom is in itself a relief.

THE RETURN OF THE GODS

The Problems of Emotion

Western students are often disconcerted in their study of Oriental psychology by the capacity of some of the "wise men of the East" for violent emotions. We have the impression that Oriental sages should be utterly calm and "controlled" under all circumstances. But this expectation is something which a certain puritanic element in the Western mind, a certain cold, intellectual desire for superhumanity and ultra-efficiency, has projected into Oriental psychology. That statement is made with certain reservations, for the same element undoubtedly exists in some of the philosophies of India, notably in Hinayana Buddhism. It must be remembered, however, that in a tropical climate vital energies, though abundant, are not particularly forceful. Chinese Buddhism is more lively, and its history contains innumerable instances of the capacity of its initiates for displays of almost elemental emotion, particularly anger. One has only to look at the demonic aspects of some of the gods and Bodhisattvas in Tibetan, Chinese, and Japanese iconography. If anyone imagines Buddhism to be a religion of pure passivity, as we understand it, he should see some of the Chinese paintings of Achala! He might also do well to visit some of the living masters of Zen Buddhism. For the art of becoming reconciled to and at ease with those aspects of natural man which correspond to storm and thunder in the natural universe is to *let* them rage. Just as there is an incomparable beauty and majesty in thunder and lightning, so also there is something awe-inspiring in the abandoned and uninhibited anger of the sage, which is no mere loss of temper or petty irritability. We remember how Jesus cast the money-changers out of the temple, and it was no cool tongue that scourged the Jews as a "generation of vipers" and the Pharisees as "whited sepulchres." This is, indeed, lack of the wrong kind of self-control, for we have to judge it from a psychological and not from an intellectual-moral point of view.

Acceptance may be both passive and violently active, and to the demon (or it may be god) of anger we say the same thing as to depression and pain, "Go ahead as much as you like, do your worst and make it a good worst." No one completely identified with his anger could ever say that, for the capacity to accept always implies a certain differentiation between the ego and the visiting demon, and thus is never the same thing as blind "possession." Only when there is possession can we call anger or passion in a certain sense immoral. But there may not always be an outward manifestation of the emotion, for here again we see that the very feeling of being free to be as angry as you like is generally sufficient release of itself. Sometimes, however, it is useful to produce an outward manifestation for the sake of effect!

False Masculinity

But here we have to face the prejudice that it is weak and effeminate to give so free a rein to the demons of emotion, for there is still a powerful element of Stoicism in our civilization, especially in the male mentality. Men are particularly averse to displaying any of the more "feminine" emotions, which, according to their version, include emotional reactions to pain and sorrow such as crying, screaming, and suffering "turns of the stomach" at unpleasant sights. Personally, I should be the last to condemn the male dislike of being "sissy," although, when carried to extremes, this dislike produces an acute "constipation" of the feeling-nature which is a common complaint among men in America. For among certain large sections of American manhood this dislike is extended to include all interest in religious, cultural and æsthetic matters, and I know many whose avoidance of these things is the purest affectation.

Inwardly this part of their being demands expression, and they deny it to their cost, for not only do they miss much that makes life more worth living; they also bring psychological ills upon themselves, the most serious of which is an abysmal failure to understand women. There is hardly another country in the world where there is so great a lack of real understanding between husbands and wives as in the United States. This is no mere empty generalization; thousands of women's clubs and sewing circles testify to the fact, for there would be no need whatever for women to herd together in this way if their home life were truly satisfactory. But the reason is an utterly false conception of manliness. When a man denies his feeling-nature he not only drives his wife to seek "culture" in women's clubs; he also drives her to seek sexual satisfaction in religion or in other men. Any primitive man would consider inability to give sexual satisfaction to his wife the greatest possible shame; but it is quite impossible to do this when one's feeling-nature is wholly repressed and when "manliness" demands that one's breath smell constantly of whisky and cigars, that one is able to make love only with phlegmatic grunts and to approach the sexual act with a directness and haste which cannot even be called bestial; it is simply thoughtless and futile, and as regards sexual relations is actually nothing more than masturbation.

To be a man at all, man has to recognize the female element in himself, for a man is no man unless he is able to give woman what she demands and needs. And she needs not just a bread-winner and a male body; she needs above all things a *companion* who can to some extent feel as she feels. This requires that the man combine in himself masculine strength and feminine grace. In this respect modern man could solve many problems of domestic life by taking a lesson from the Hindu "book of marriage," the *Kama Sutra*.[13] The art of *Kama*, the use of the senses, is an essential part of the old-fashioned Hindu education, but we fail almost completely to teach young men anything that will be of use in married life, quite apart from the art of sexuality. We cannot be strict Stoics without being celibate. But the Stoic philosophy does not recognize that control of the emotions is in no sense being without emotions; controlling an automobile is not keeping it locked up in the garage. You cannot begin to control emotions unless you first let yourself be free to use them, and the difficulty of keeping them within reasonable bounds is increased by merely repressive control. For this reason there are thousands of supposedly well-educated people who behave worse than children when moved by powerful emotion, having no understanding and above all no love for the feminine in themselves. Small wonder, then, that modern man has to become reconciled to his unconscious under the form of the feminine *anima*! His psychological problem is primarily to make a successful marriage within himself—a marriage between ego and *anima*, between conscious reason and unconscious nature, in which there must be love, companionship, and understanding. Failure to realize this inner relationship is always reflected outwardly in the divided home where man is man and woman is woman "and never the twain shall meet." They have separate friends, separate interests, separate bedrooms and separate souls; this is not marriage; it is a business partnership for manufacturing children.

WOMAN UNSATISFIED

The problem for modern woman is rather different. There is a powerful male element in her, and the danger is not that she may repress it but that she may be possessed by it. For the result of our current lack of relationship between the sexes is not, as one might expect, that men become increasingly manly and women increasingly womanly. Both tend to become neuter, but in different ways. When men have no real use for femininity women forget their arts; they cultivate one another's company to the virtual exclusion of men, and this can only be done safely by those who have fulfilled their life with men and by children. The result is masculinity among women, feminism (a gross misnomer), a tendency to intellectualism, competition with men in business and that hard-boiled bridge-playing, cocktail-drinking mentality which is only golf, whisky, and cigars wearing skirts. Thus the drift in both sexes is to a false masculinity for which absence of feeling among men is very much to blame; and absence of feeling is simply the lack of recognizing one's own gods and demons. When conscious reason is predominant all values become strictly "practical" and intellectual, while feeling is degraded to mere sensation. It would not be so bad, however, if this cult of the "practical" and intellectual were what it tries to be. But when women try to be practical in this new sense they lose their inborn reason which, in the past, has always kept men with their feet on the earth and made them realize their responsibilities to their homes and their children.

Indeed, we call the unconscious irrational, but really it is so-called reason that is crazy. The fault is not with reason in itself but with the conscious, intellectual idea of what reason ought to be, namely a mathematical operation which excludes feeling and the demands of physical being. True woman understands these things; if she did not the children would never be fed (much less the husband) and the home would never be habitable—which may be proved by visiting the homes of those "practical" wives who go into business, socialism, cultural ideals, and other idealistic, theoretical, and nebulous matters. The curious thing is that such behavior never achieves the desired result, and it is not uncommon that *real* women converse far more intelligently about literature, music, the arts, politics, religion, and all cultural affairs than their home-neglecting sisters who go out to acquire these very things. They are so busy *trying* to be clever that they have no time simply to be clever.

THE FEMININE PRINCIPLE

It is almost as if our civilization were suffering from an eclipse of the feminine principle, and it is no mere chance that this coincides with the extreme of self-consciousness. Traditionally, the dark side of life, the unknown, the mysterious was always female; its great symbol is water, the mysterious depth out of which life appears, and because of its passivity and depth, water has always been accounted feminine. Therefore for us the words of Lao Tzu have a special point:[14]

> He who knows the masculine and yet keeps to the feminine
> Will become a channel drawing all the world towards it.

And again:

> Man when living is soft and tender; when dead he is hard and tough. All animals and plants when living are tender and fragile; when dead they become withered and dry. Therefore it is said: the hard and tough are parts of death; the soft and tender are parts of life. This is the reason why the soldiers when they are too tough cannot carry the day; the tree when it is too tough will break. The position of the strong and great is low, and the position of the weak and tender is high.

In other words, acceptance as a feminine technique re-awakens our lost "better half" and makes us whole, for acceptance is the way of the tree that is weak and tender—like the willow. Under the weight of snow its boughs bend down and cast the snow off; but on the boughs of the knotted, rigid pine the snow piles up and up until they crack. This is called stooping to conquer.

> The best soldier is not soldierly;
> The best fighter is not ferocious;
> The best conqueror does not take part in war;
> The best employer of men keeps himself below them.
> This is called the virtue of not contending;
> This is called the ability of using men;
> This is called the supremacy of consorting with heaven.

Every true woman knows the virtue of not contending by which she gets her own way, for

> The highest goodness is like water. Water is beneficent to all things but does not contend. It stays in places which others despise. Therefore it is near Tao.

Cutting it, you can leave no wound because it always yields; grasping it, you cannot hold it because it always falls through your fingers. You can only hold it by making a cup of your hands. Now water is a symbol of life and a cup of acceptance and a sword of aggressiveness. The cup is also a feminine symbol, and of this Lao Tzu says:

Clay is moulded into vessels
And because of the space where nothing exists we are able to use them as vessels.
Doors and windows are cut out in the walls of a house,
And because they are empty spaces, we are able to use them.

For acceptance is emptiness in the Buddhist sense of *sunyata*, which is sometimes likened to a crystal or a mirror. "The perfect man," says Chuang Tzu, "employs his mind as a mirror. It grasps nothing; it refuses nothing; it receives, but does not keep." So, too, a crystal takes into itself whatever lies around it. When you hold it up before a busy street, it holds the busy street; when you hold it up before the empty sky, it seems to hold nothing—but only because it is reflecting the emptiness of the sky. What is its own real nature? It is neither full nor void; it is beyond all opposites, and thus is a symbol of spiritual freedom. This reminds me of the conversation between the Buddhist sage Tozan and one of his disciples. Said the disciple, "Cold and heat alternately come and go, and how can one escape them?" Tozan answered, "Why not go where there is neither cold nor heat?" "Where," persisted the disciple, "is the place where there is neither cold nor heat?" "When the cold season is here, we all feel cold. When the hot season is here we all feel hot."[15]

A curious feature of the quest for freedom is the appearance of a snag just as you think you are getting somewhere. The snag appears for the very reason that you think you *are* getting somewhere, for the essential point of spirituality, the point so difficult to grasp, is that it is not a question of *going* at all. You cannot get the freedom of the spirit by climbing up to it; it is not reached by any kind of ladder, for otherwise it would be possible to describe a specific technique by which wisdom and enlightenment can be "obtained" and the whole matter would be as apparently simple as buying a ticket and taking a train. But the steps and stages are not laid out in black and white, and there are no fixed rules and regulations the mere observance of which will achieve the desired result. It is very much like learning to love someone. You cannot look up a book of rules and find out how to love, although many such books have been written.

Now the practice of any kind of technique is *going* somewhere, yes, even the technique of acceptance. If this is true, it will be asked why anyone should go to the trouble of talking about it at all; if even the technique of acceptance will not, of itself, achieve the desired object, why introduce it? Because, according to the proverb, the longest way round is the shortest way home. It seems to be necessary to try to discover the secret by going somewhere in order to learn that this can never be done. The path always takes you round in a circle, back to the place where you stand. It is the parable of the Prodigal Son over again, and the Buddhists describe it as the journey of a lunatic all over the world in search of his head, which he had never lost. There is no doubt at all that from one point of view the technique of acceptance actually works, but it is always partial. It is admirable for solving an immediate problem, in instances of pain, depression, and sorrow, but there is always something it leaves unsolved, for there remains a subtle, indefinable and elusive inner discontent.

THE LONGING FOR GOD

This is truly a "divine discontent" for I believe it to be what the mystics describe as the yearning of the soul for God; as St. Augustine says, "Thou hast made us for Thyself, therefore we may not rest anywhere save in Thee." By a hundred different techniques we can adjust the details of our lives and make ourselves happy in the superficial sense of having nothing specific to be unhappy about. But techniques can only deal with details, with separate parts; something different is required to transform one's attitude to life as a whole, and to transform the whole of one's life. Without this transformation the real unhappiness remains, expressing itself in all manner of disguises, finding innumerable substitutes for God which do not work because they are always *partial* things. They are, as it were, the parts of God, but not the whole of Him. Technique can find these parts; it can find acceptance, wealth, pleasure, experience, knowledge, and all the lesser gods and demons of the unknown realms of the soul. But even when all these many parts are brought together, there is still something which no technical trick or device can discover, and this is the whole which is greater than the sum of its parts.

Those who have followed partial techniques know that in a life where there is nothing special to be unhappy about there is a kind of barrenness; it is like a wheel without a center, or a perfect lamp without a light. There is nothing to supply any creative fire. Everything is going just as it should go; the daily routine may be a little dull, but it is by no means unbearable. Certainly there are troubles, but nothing overwhelming. As for one's own character, well, that is quite normal. There are no serious neurotic troubles and no moral defects. For the most part life is quite agreeable and if death comes at the end of it, that is a matter of course for which nature will prepare us; when the time comes to die we shall be tired and ready to go. That is not a happy life, even though it may be contented; it is simple vegetation. There is not that joyous response of the individual to the universe which is the essence of spirituality, which expresses itself in religious worship and adoration. I suppose there must have been times in everyone's life when there has been such a response, even for a short moment. In those moments most of us like to be alone, for we are afraid to let others see us become so childish. After all, we are dignified adults and it would not do at all for Mr. Cornelius Pomp, president of Grand International Railways, Inc., to be seen dancing wildly around on a hilltop in the middle of the night for sheer joy at seeing the stars. But I have no doubt there was an occasion when Mr. Pomp, in the dim recesses of his being, felt very much like doing this but could not unbend.

It is a symptom of our spiritual phlegmatism and torpidity that the dance is no longer a part of our ritual and that we worship in churches which, as often as not, resemble cattle-pens where people sit in rows and pray by leaning forward in their seats and mumbling. Sometimes people try to get away from this stiffness by putting on short pants and running out to the woods for community dancing and the cultivation of response to nature, and there are other people who try to make their prayers sincere by groveling on their knees and whimpering. This is another case of trying to make the tail wag the dog. The first essential is to feel the joy; the response follows of its own accord, but you cannot get the joy by slavishly imitating the response. In fact we first have to feel as St. Francis felt in writing his Canticle to the Sun, which is perhaps the most superb expression of the joy of spiritual freedom that was ever written:

> Praise to my Lord for all His creatures;
> for our brother Sun who bringeth us day
> and light, and showeth Thee unto us.

> Praise to my Lord for our sister Moon
> and for the Stars hung bright and lovely in Heaven.

> Praise to my Lord for our brother Wind
> and for Air and Clouds, Calm and all Weather
> whereby Thou maintainest life in all beings.

> Praise to my Lord for our sister Water,
> useful and lowly, precious and clear.

> Praise to my Lord for our brother Fire,
> mighty and strong, by whom Thou makest
> for us light in darkness.

Praise to my Lord for our mother Earth
who doth uphold and teach us, and bringeth
forth in many colors both fruit and flowers.

Praise to my Lord for sister Death,
from whom none can flee. Blessed are
those who find themselves in Thy most
Holy Will, for Death shall not harm them.

Oh all ye creatures, praise and bless my
Lord, and be thankful, and serve Him in
great humility.

THE ECSTASY OF CREATION

This hymn of happiness is more than a hymn of acceptance, for it includes not only sun and moon, fire and water,
life and death; it includes also God, and those who find God
are happy because they share in the ecstasy of creation.
They, too, know the answer to that eternal question of philosophy, "*Why* does the universe exist?" They know that it
exists for an almost childlike reason—for play, or what the
Hindus called *lila* (which is nearly our own word "lilt").[1]
Chesterton points out that when a child sees you do something wonderful, it asks you to do it again and again. So
too he says that God made the earth and told it to move
round the sun, and when it had moved round once He was
pleased and said, "Do it again." He has been saying it ever
since. To some this may seem sentimental, to others ir-
reverent, and to yet others absurd, for how can one say
that all the cruelty, destruction, and anguish of life is play?
And if it is play, is not God like a thoughtless child who
picks a butterfly to pieces to watch it struggle? But for
what other reason could it have been said that when the

foundations of the earth were laid "the morning stars sang together, and all the sons of God shouted for joy"?[2]

But those who ask this question about the cruelty of God's play are expecting him who answers to make excuses for God, to "justify the ways of God to man," and as Lao Tzu has tersely and aptly said, "Those who justify themselves do not convince." Should we ask and expect the universe to conform with our standards of good behavior and doubt the existence of God in all things because He does not observe the ordinary standards of middle-class humanitarian morality? We think of God as a meek, kindly old gentleman, or else as an infinitely powerful but essentially nebulous spirit of pure love, by which we mean pure dotingness. But, as Edwin Arnold has written, ——

> It slayeth and it saveth, nowise moved
>   Except unto the working out of doom;
> Its threads are Love and Life; and Death and Pain
>   The shuttles of its loom.

The dissertations on the so-called "Problem of Evil," which has so much worried Christian theologians, are nothing more than an attempt to apologize for the Deity, and such attempts invariably indicate lack of faith. And faith in God, faith in life, faith in nature, is the important thing; that faith is the very key to freedom of the spirit.

THE FAITH OF ABANDONMENT

Faith is not blind belief, and it is certainly not mere intellectual assent to the proposition that God exists. Nor is it trusting that life will work out "all right" *in spite* of its tribulations. Faith is not hope. From one point of view faith is the most illogical thing in the world; it is trusting life *because* of its tribulations; it is the sense of love and wonder before the mystery of a God who is both Creator and Destroyer, love and terror, life and death, angel and demon, sage and fool, man and worm. There are those who ask why they should be expected to have faith of so unconditional a kind in a universe which takes with one hand what it gives with the other, and the answer suggests a story about Thomas Carlyle. There was a woman who wrote him a long dissertation which ended with the words, "In short, I accept the universe." "My God!" said Carlyle. "She'd better!" For the truth is simply that without faith we are forever bashing our heads against an immovable wall. No self-deception, no trick of reason or science, no magic, no amount of self-reliance can make us independent of the universe and enable us to escape its destructive aspect. Pain is a fact and no amount of wishful theology can explain it away with promises and apologies for its existence in a universe whose God is supposed to be "love." At the same time no amount of acceptance can make away with our fundamental horror of pain in its more extreme forms. But, even so, faith can never be real faith if it is half-hearted, if we think that it is merely a question of the "best policy," of the best means to make an intolerable situation a little more bearable.

God, life, and the universe keep their two aspects whatever we may try to think about them, and continue their play in all its love and all its cruelty. Faith means that we give ourselves to it absolutely and utterly, without making conditions of any kind, that we abandon ourselves to God without asking anything in return, save that our abandonment to Him may make us feel more keenly the lilt of His playing. This abandonment is the freedom of the spirit.[3]

That is the only promise which can be given for faith, but what a promise! It means that we share in the ecstasy of His creation and His destruction, and experience the mystery and the freedom of His power in all the aspects of life, in both the heights of pleasure and the depths of pain. It may seem illogical, but those who have once shared in this mystery have a gratitude that knows no bounds and are able to say again that God is Love, though with an altogether new meaning.

THE MAN AND THE MEANS

But we cannot make a technique of abandonment, for at once a snag arises. It is the same snag that stands between partial and total acceptance and may be described in a number of different ways. Fundamentally it is the old problem of lifting oneself up by one's own belt and is perhaps most aptly put in the Chinese saying that "when the wrong man uses the right means, the right means work in the wrong way." The "right means" are all forms of technique—acceptance, abandonment, and what you will; the "wrong man" is, generally speaking, oneself. We are "wrong" in the sense that we are unhappy, that we are without faith and have no freedom of spirit. The problem is therefore how the wrong man can become the right man when all the available means for so doing are bound to work in the wrong way. In other words, a man desires to change himself. Now a man is what he is, and his desires are according to his nature. If he is a "bad" man, his desires will be bad, even though one of them is that he shall become better. We discover this by asking *why* he wants to become better. The underlying motive for improvement is tainted because the man who entertains it is bad; he wants to become better out of self-interest, because in his pride he wishes to escape from the reproach of being bad. If this is pointed out to him, he will then ask whether he ought simply to accept his badness. And if we again ask him *why* he wants to accept his badness, we discover that he wants to accept it in order to escape from it. He is caught whichever way he turns because the means he adopts, his behavior, his ideas, his religion, are always *his*, and he will always use them according to his capacity and his nature. They are like so many different suits of clothes; he may wear rags, ermine, tweeds, or skins; he may walk, run, skip, or trot; he may whisper, shout, sing, or talk—but he himself remains the same since he is the cause and not the consequence of his actions.

Let us put it in another way. Supposing that we decide to accept the dark side of life, the unconscious and the conflict between the unconscious and the ego, there is still one thing that by this means we do not accept—our desire to escape from it. Until that desire is accepted our acceptance is always an indirect attempt to escape. Here we meet the problem of St. Michael and the Dragon again. Christian morality taught us to overcome the dark side of life by fighting it; psychology would have us overcome it by acceptance, but in fact these are both ways of *overcoming* it, which means getting rid of it and escaping it. Thus the way of acceptance as distinct from the way of fighting is apt to make a new Dragon out of St. Michael.

INFINITE REGRESSION

There is also the problem of the relation between nature and the ego. If we accept the universe and subordinate ourselves to it, if, instead of trying to live life, we let life live us, we are accepting one aspect of life only to deny another—the aggressive, self-asserting ego in which life has manifested itself. Acceptance is indeed the feminine way, but it cannot be practiced at the expense of the masculine. It seems, therefore, that what we need is, as it were, a higher type of acceptance that includes both acceptance and escape, faith and suspicion, self-abandonment and egotism, surrender and aggressiveness, the Dragon and St. Michael. But even this does not quite solve the problem—indeed, it is as far from a solution as ever—because we are starting out upon an infinite regression. We are becoming hopelessly involved in a vicious circle, for as soon as we set up the notion of an acceptance which takes in both accepting and escaping we have two pairs of opposites instead of one. We begin with the opposition of acceptance$_1$ vs. escape; but we then get acceptance$_2$ vs. acceptance$_1$-vs.-escape—a psychological monstrosity which can continue indefinitely.

At first sight the problem of the vicious circle may seem purely mathematical and remote from experience. But in fact it is only a rather complicated way of expressing the fundamental conundrum that those who search for happiness do not find it. It is again the problem of the donkey with the carrot suspended before his nose from a stick that is fastened to his own collar. If he chases it, using the aggressive technique, he does not catch it; if he stands still, using the passive technique, he still does not catch it. What can he do? The poor creature is apparently quite helpless. Of course, it will be said that any attempt to answer such riddles is an easy way to go crazy. This is very true, and for just the same reasons it will be discovered that any attempt to discover happiness is also an easy way to go crazy, and the world today is a crazy place just because people are trying to do it. We are a collection of people running wildly round in circles in frantic pursuit of our own selves, and the picture is not particularly edifying. Yes, if we could see ourselves from a psychological standpoint we should think we had walked into bedlam. We should see men running away from their shadows, men trying to jump off the ground by tugging at their shoelaces, men trying to see their own eyes and kiss their own lips. It is like trying to mend a hole in one part of a handkerchief by taking a patch from another. For the trouble is that all our schemes, systems, and devices are *partial*. It is as if we ourselves were the hole in the handkerchief; we see some other part of the handkerchief and think how pleasant it would be to fill our emptiness by acquiring it. So we cut it out and fill ourselves, only to find that we are now the new hole—the invisible blind-spot in the universe.[4]

THE SQUIRREL-CAGE OF DUALITY

That which we call God can only be known intimately by *total* acceptance, because freedom by its very nature cannot be limited. Therefore we may say that when you consider yourself free to accept but not to escape, this is not freedom. But the human mind is so constructed that it cannot imagine total acceptance; our intellect is such that it must think in dualities—this and not that, that and not this. It is a see-saw; one end must be up and the other down; both ends cannot be up at the same time and down at the same time. Therefore freedom of the spirit demands the interference of some factor over and above the human intellect. For not only is the intellect unable to conceive of this totality, it is also unable to appreciate its value, arguing that in "abolishing" dualism you destroy all values, give sanction to the wildest libertinism and in fact require nothing more of the spiritual man than that he should do as he likes. (Somehow we are reminded of St. Augustine's precept, "Love, and do as you will.") The same objection is raised to the Oriental idea of God as the Self of the universe, the One Reality and true self of all creatures, forms, activities, thoughts, and substances. It is argued that if everything is God, then God is nothing—on the principle of W. S. Gilbert's line, "When everybody's somebody, then no one's anybody."

The Oriental philosophies of Vedanta, Taoism, and Mahayana Buddhism do not, however, involve this *reductio ad absurdum*, because to say that all things are God is not quite the same as saying that everything is one thing; in fact it is not even remotely the same. In their view God is not *a thing*, and they do not abolish all differences by reducing individual shapes and forms to a single, infinite formlessness. For God is not the One as *distinct from* the Many, nor unity as distinct from diversity.[5] We cannot begin to understand the Oriental view of God until we can conceive of a "One" that can include both unity and diversity, which can at the same time be God and a speck of dust or a human being with equal reality. In this sense it might be said that the oneness of things is revealed in their multiplicity and diversity. Such paradoxes are inevitable when we try to approach non-duality from the intellectual point of view. This is true not only of intellect, for the way of acceptance which we have already described involves much more than mere thinking; nevertheless it is just as liable to be involved in this squirrel-cage of duality.

The problems of duality are clearly stated in the Christian faith, but they often pass unrecognized under the symbols in which they are contained. The story of the Fall, of the eating of the fruit of the Tree of Good and Evil, describes man's involvement in the vicious circle—a condition in which, of his own power, he is able to do nothing good that is not vitiated by evil. In this condition it may be said that "all good deeds are done for the love of gain," that is, with a purely self-interested motive, because "honesty is the best policy." Every advance in morality is counterbalanced by the growth of repressed evil in the unconscious, for morality has to be imposed by law and wherever there is compulsion there is repression of instinctual urges. Indeed, the very formulation of the ideal of righteousness suggests and aggravates its opposite. Thus St. Paul says, "I had not known lust, except the law had said, Thou shalt not covet." So, too, Lao Tzu remarks in the *Tao Te Ching*:

When the great Tao is lost, spring forth benevolence and righteousness.
When wisdom and sagacity arise, there are great hypocrites.
When family relations are no longer harmonious, we have filial children and devoted parents.
When a nation is in confusion and disorder, patriots are recognized.
Where Tao is, equilibrium is. When Tao is lost, out come all the differences of things.

Trans. Ch'u Ta-kao.

It is not surprising, therefore, that Christian doctrine follows St. Paul in saying that salvation for fallen man is unattainable by law alone, which is to say by technique. For this is not only a question of morality. So long as man attempts to save himself by the mere observance of moral, spiritual, or psychological *law* he is involved in the vicious circle of duality.

THE ACCEPTANCE OF GRACE

The motivating power of the vicious circle is pride. In Christian terms we should say that man is not willing to be saved as he is; he feels that it is necessary for him to do something about it, to earn salvation by his own self-made spirituality and righteousness. The Grace of God is offered freely to all, but through pride man will not accept it. He cannot bear the thought that he is absolutely powerless to lift himself up and that the only chance of salvation is simply to accept something which is offered as freely to the saint as to the sinner. If nothing can be done to earn this Grace it seems to set all man's self-imposed ideals at naught; he has to confess himself impotent, and this is more than he can bear. So the gift of Grace is tacitly ignored, and man goes on trying to manufacture it for himself.[6]

When it is said that man will not let himself be saved as he is, this is another way of saying that he will not accept himself as he is; subtly he gets around this simple act by making a technique out of acceptance, setting it up as something which he *should* do in order to be a "good boy." And as soon as acceptance is made a question of *doing* and technique we have the vicious circle. True acceptance is not something to be *attained*; it is not an ideal to be sought after—a state of soul which can be possessed and acquired, which we can add to ourselves in order to increase our spiritual stature. If another paradox may be forgiven, true acceptance is accepting yourself as you are NOW, at this moment, before you have even begun to make yourself different by accepting yourself.[7] In other words, as soon as we try to make the ideal state of mind called "acceptance" something different from the state of mind which we have at this moment, this is the pride which makes it so difficult to accept what we are now, the barrier that stands between man and that which we call God or Tao.

But when it is suggested that we should find union with God here and now at this very moment, everyone is outraged and begins to make excuses. "After all, how can *we* attain such sublime understanding at this moment? We are unprepared. We are not good enough. We shall have to do all kinds of things first. We must meditate and train ourselves in religious discipline, and then perhaps after many years we shall be fit and worthy to attain that greatest of all attainments." But this is surely a peculiar form of blindness and false pride, masquerading as humility. We see God every time we open our eyes; we inhale Him at every breath; we use His strength in every movement of a finger; we think Him in every thought, although we may not think *of* Him, and we taste Him in every bite of food. This is an old story to those who have studied the wisdom of the East, but still the search goes on, a search for something we have never lost, something which is staring us right in the face, a search which the Buddhists sometimes describe as "hiding loot in one's pocket and declaring oneself innocent." It is difficult just because it is too easy, for man finds it so hard to climb down from his high horse and accept that which *is*, freely and unreservedly. Small wonder, then, that we are advised to become again as little children, who have an inconvenient way of drawing attention to obvious things which the adult mind cannot or will not see. For spiritual understanding is not a reward given to you for being a great person; you cannot acquire it any more than you can acquire the wind and the stars. But you can open your eyes and see it.

THE DWELLER ON THE THRESHOLD

Now in this true acceptance of oneself there is a mystery, for, as the Pythagoreans say, "Know thyself, and thou wilt know the universe and the gods." The mystery is that something so apparently simple and lowly as oneself as it is at this moment can contain so great a treasure. But that is the peculiarity of divine Grace; it is always found where it would least be expected, for, in the words of Lao Tzu, Tao "seeks, like water, the lowly level which men abhor." And so it happens that the very thing we are forever struggling to get away from, to outgrow, to change, and to escape, is the very thing which holds the much desired secret. That is why there is a vicious circle, why our search for happiness is this frantic running around, pursuing in ignorance that which we are trying to flee. We are running away from our front in order to catch up with our back, with the result that, for us, happiness is always somewhere in the future, just round the corner perhaps, but always beyond. Ourselves and our situation as they are at this moment contain the whole secret, but when we try to accept them in the technical way we are still going on with the circular chase; we are trying to add to them the virtue of acceptance so that we do not have to face them as they are, without their acceptance and with all their shortcomings, their conflicts, their desires to escape, their impotence, and their sins. We catch a glimpse of them from time to time in all their nakedness and run from them as fast as we can go, trying to improve them, spiritualize them and in a thousand other ways hide such terrible nudity. Naturally we deceive ourselves and begin to have fanciful pictures of ourselves as we are. But when these pictures are torn away we meet again the unedifying and fearful sight of our real selves, and it seems impossible that the great treasure can have anything to do with such a degraded state of affairs.

From one point of view this sight of our true selves is the dreaded Dweller on the Threshold, the monster which all initiates into the divine mysteries have to face on the brink of their enlightenment. But the Dweller on the Threshold is the face of God seen from *this* side of the brink; you pass over the brink if you can call Him by His real name, though it needs a profound humility to utter it. For to accept the Grace of God as you are now, without any "improvements" and dressing up in more respectable clothes, is to realize that all the cherished ambitions of self-interest, all your efforts to make yourself great, are vain. You have to come down to the level of worms and dust which have not a particle of your cleverness and yet exist by the Grace of God. Most people know this from childhood, and yet never can be simple enough to recognize it, for "which of you by taking thought can add one cubit unto his stature? . . . Consider the lilies of the field, how they grow; they toil not, neither do they spin: and yet I say unto you, that even Solomon in all his glory was not arrayed like one of these. Wherefore, if God so clothe the grass of the field, which to-day is, and to-morrow is cast into the oven, shall he not much more clothe you, O ye of little faith?"[8] It would be well for those who struggle so hard in the squirrel-cage of duality to be spiritual, to accept, to find wisdom, and to be happy to remember occasionally those words, "Which of you by taking thought can add one cubit unto his stature?"

THE MEANING OF HAPPINESS

THE RELIGIOUS PROBLEM OF MODERN MAN

But familiarity breeds contempt. Modern man is now seeking in all manner of new religions, in the psychology of the unconscious and in the wisdom of Asia what has always been in the teaching of Christ and the symbolism of the Church. Yet we cannot blame him, so much has the Christian religion been dragged in the mud. Most of its teachers have long forgotten the meaning of its symbols, even if they ever knew them, and the events in the life of the spirit which they describe have been placed at the safe distance of bygone history. Moreover its Bible is such a vast collection of conflicting ideas that Christians, accepting *all* of it as the word of God, have often fallen into the absurdity of trying to incorporate the legalistic morality of the Jews[9] into their own faith with the fantastic result that many forms of Protestantism are much more Jewish than Christian. They try to interpret the Sermon on the Mount in the same spirit as the Ten Commandments, whereas if they had ever read St. Paul they would realize their utter difference. (Curiously enough, there are times when even St. Paul seems unable to shake off his hereditary legalism and realize the full implications of his own faith.) But in Christianity this legalistic moralism has been carried to such extremes of sanctimonious gloom that for thousands the very word "religion" means little more than doing exactly what you don't like. So often have the words "God" and "Christ" been said with a frown in the voice or with a type of intense seriousness in which there is no room for humor or beauty that they are apt to cause a deadness of heart instead of a thrill. There is hardly any other religion in the world with quite this depressive atmosphere, and even in Christianity it is

136

confined mainly to Protestantism—to the spiritual descendants of Calvin, Luther, Knox, and Wesley. It is small wonder, therefore, that people of spirit turn to the more colorful faiths of Catholicism (if they wish to remain Christian), Buddhism, Hinduism, Theosophy or, if they are of a more scientific mentality, to one of the many psychological systems of modern times. I even know those who acknowledge themselves Pagans, Sun-worshipers, and Polytheists.

But Christianity is our traditional faith; it is in our blood and bones. Therefore it is possible and very desirable that the wisdom of Asia and the psychology of the unconscious will bring its treasures to light again and interpret them in a way that will give us an altogether new zest for it. Until I had studied the religions of the East for some years the teaching of Christ and the symbols of Christianity had no real meaning for me. But I do not mean to suggest that a study of Oriental faiths is essential for an understanding of Christianity. For my own part, I believe that my understanding would have been much the same had I read Eckhart, Augustine, à Kempis, Berdyaev, and others of their caliber instead of the sages of India and China. But there is an increasing interest in the wisdom of the East among us which will take its own course and to which many will turn before they ever understand Christianity as anything more than a set of inhibitions and outworn dogmas. Of all the new religions and ways of life that have been evolved in the West, Christianity is almost alone in understanding a way out of the vicious circle of dualism, but it is difficult to see how that way can appeal to thousands of thinking men and women unless they can approach Christianity with somewhat changed conceptions of God and the soul. For, as Jung so often points out, the difficulty for modern man with his rationalistic background is to believe in Christianity as a system of theology. As he writes in *Modern Man in Search of a Soul*:

People no longer feel themselves to be redeemed by the death of Christ; they cannot believe—they cannot compel themselves to believe, however happy they may deem the man who has a belief. Sin has for them become something quite relative: what is evil for one is good for another. After all, why should not Buddha be in the right also? (p. 268)

Indeed, we may say of modern man's attitude to religion as a whole that he has little patience with doctrines that are beyond objective proof and that seem to him, perhaps arbitrarily, to be stretching his credulity. But if he can be shown that there is a psychological approach to Christianity almost independent of doctrine as such, in which doctrines are taken as symbols of spiritual experiences, this may perhaps be the foundation for a wholly new attitude to religion in the Western world. This is the point of view from which we shall approach the doctrines of the Orient—a point of view which many Easterners have adopted and among whom we must number the Buddha himself. He valued only immediate personal experiences and when questioned upon the ultimate mysteries of the universe answered only with "silence—and a finger pointing the way."

Although that freedom of the spirit which is known through the total acceptance of life and of oneself can never be contained in any form of words and ideas, it is most clearly expressed in the ancient wisdom of Asia. In Hindu Vedanta, Mahayana Buddhism, and Taoism we find a view of life which comes as near as anything to a description of that inner experience which reveals, as the Japanese Buddhist Hakuin wrote, that

> This very earth is the Lotus Land of Purity,
> And this very body is the body of Buddha.

The approach to this understanding began independently in both India and China; after a period of centuries the two streams merged and, to my own mind, achieved their fulfilment in China some twelve hundred years ago. In studying this wisdom it is important to follow its historical development, both to grasp the continuity of experience and to see how close a resemblance there is between the growth in history and the growth of that same experience in the mind of the individual. Bear always in mind that the doctrines of these ancient religions are the symbols of inward, personal experiences rather than attempts to describe metaphysical truth. The important thing is not whether the doctrine contains an objective statement of fact about the universe; it is to discover what inward experience, what state of mind or attitude to life would lead human beings to think in that way. For the wisdom of the East has a strictly practical aim which is not mere knowledge *about* the universe; it aims at a transformation of the individual and of his feeling for life through experience rather than belief. This experience is psychological or spiritual, not metaphysical, and except in certain specialized fields has no relation to occultism or to what we understand in the West as philosophy. (See above, Ch. 2, pp. 42-5 and Ch. 3, p. 81.)

VEDANTA AND THE UPANISHADS

Some eight hundred years before the birth of Christ the sages of India began to instruct their disciples with a number of collected sayings and parables known as the Upanishads. No one knows who first uttered them, though from time to time some of them are attributed to Yajnavalkya, of whom Geden writes, "If the name represents a real individuality, and is not merely a title under whose shelter many convergent thoughts and reasonings have found expression, Yajnavalkya may claim a place with the greatest thinkers of the world or of any age." The Upanishads are the foundation of what was subsequently known as Vedanta (*veda-anta*), which is to say the "end" or fulfilment of the Vedas, the Vedas being the earliest of all Hindu scriptures. With matchless economy and beauty of language the Upanishads speak in a number of different ways of Brahman, the One Reality which is expressed in all the manifold forms, objects, activities, and living beings of the universe. Thus it is said in the *Katha Upanishad*:[1]

As the wind, though one, takes on new forms in whatever it enters; the Spirit, though one, takes new forms in whatever that lives. He is within all, and is also outside. . . . There is one

Ruler, the Spirit that is in all things, who transforms His one form into many. Only the wise who see Him in their souls attain the joy eternal.

And again:

From His life comes the universe, and in His life the universe moves. In His majesty is the terror of thunder. Those who know this attain immortality. From fear of Him fire burns and from fear of Him the sun shines. From fear of Him the clouds and winds, and death itself, move on their way.

And in the *Mundaka Upanishad*:

From Him comes all life and mind and the senses of all life. From Him comes space and light, air and fire and water, and this earth that holds us all. . . . From Him comes the sun, and the source of all fire is the sun. From him comes the moon, and from this comes the rain and all herbs that grow upon earth. And man comes from Him, and man unto woman gives seed: and thus an infinity of beings comes from the Spirit supreme.

But what is the exact relation between Brahman and His creatures? Is it the same relation of Creator to creature that we find in the Christian and Islamic conceptions, or is it the pantheistic relation of participation, in which the creature is a part of God, where God is one with the universe? The answer is given in the *Chandogya Upanishad*:

All this universe is in truth Brahman. He is the beginning and end and life of all. As such, in silence, give unto Him adoration. . . . There is a Spirit that is mind and life, light and truth and vast spaces. He contains all works and desires and all perfumes and all tastes. He enfolds the whole universe, and in silence is loving to all. This is the Spirit that is in my heart, smaller than a grain of rice, or a grain of barley, or a grain of mustard-seed. . . . This is the Spirit that is in my heart, greater than the earth, greater than the sky, greater than heaven itself, greater than all these worlds.

At first it sounds almost like pure pantheism, but later in the same Upanishad the master says, "An invisible and subtle essence is the Spirit of the whole universe. That is Reality. That is Truth. *Thou art That.*" The master does not tell his disciple that he is a *part* of Brahman; he tells him that he *is* Brahman, and if we are to give this doctrine a label we must say that it is not pantheism but pan*en*theism.[2] In the same way St. Catherine of Genoa says, "My *me* is God, nor do I know my selfhood save in Him," and again, "My Being is God, not by simple participation, but by a true transformation of my Being."[3]

Therefore the phrase "That art thou" (*tat tvam asi*) is the first, fundamental principle of Vedanta arising from the second, that all things without exception are Brahman, not by participation, for Brahman is one and indivisible. Hence Vedanta is also known as the system of Advaita (literally "not two") or non-duality, and non-duality in philosophy is the natural expression of total acceptance in psychology. Every object, being and activity is Brahman in His (or Its) entirety, for Brahman alone *is*—the "One-without-a-second." But, it will be asked, if Brahman is the only reality, why do things appear to be separate, why do we human beings feel that we are separate egos and how is it that we are ignorant of our identity with Brahman? This, according to Vedanta, is *maya*—a word grossly misunderstood by most Western interpreters of Hindu thought, who translate it simply as "illusion." As we have already shown, the original meaning of *maya* was "trick" or "device," and it is sometimes described as the creative power of Brahman. Woodroffe describes it thus in his *Shakti and Shakta*:[4]

Maya is not rightly rendered Illusion. In the first place it is conceived as a real Power of Being and as such is one with Full Reality. The Full, free of all illusion, experiences the engendering of the finite centers and the centers themselves in and as Its own changeless partless Self. . . . Even God cannot have man's mode of knowledge and enjoyment without becoming man. He by and as His Power does become man and yet remains Himself. Man is Power in limited form as Avidya (ignorance). The Lord is unlimited Power as Maya. (p. 44)

In other words, if man has the experience of separateness, this experience also is Brahman since there is nothing other than Brahman. *Maya* is not illusion as against reality, for in the Vedantist conception there is nothing apart from Reality which may be set over against it. Thus we may say that while there is no actual separateness from Brahman, there is certainly an *experience* of separateness, and this experience is real even though it is incomplete and relative. *Maya* is therefore only translatable as "illusion" in regard to the actual existence of separateness from Brahman; but as the experience of separateness *maya* is creative power, for that experience is the device whereby Brahman manifests Himself as creatures who act on their own initiative.

But does this imply that though we may have a real experience, say, of a tree and a mountain as separate things, those two are not there at all, that while the experience may be real it has no real object to be known as a tree and a mountain? Is our imagination simply conjuring up these forms by Brahman's power out of a vast and formless infinitude of sameness and uniformity? Do the Vedantins imply that when we have ascended from the partial experience of *maya* to the total experience of Brahman, we are conscious only of this infinite oneness and have no longer any perception of trees and mountains? Although many texts would seem to answer these questions in the affirmative, I cannot see that this is a true interpretation of the Upanishads or of the fundamental principle of non-duality. For it is not at all consistent with that principle to identify Brahman with infinite unity as distinct from finite diversity, with formlessness as distinct from form. If Brahman is truly non-dual, He cannot be the infinite as opposed to the finite. But when we say that a man, a mountain, or a tree *is* Brahman, we are not denying that it is a man, a mountain, or a tree. Conversely, if such objects are real, this does not involve their separateness from Brahman and in no way denies the statement that Brahman is the only reality. If by saying that man *is* Brahman we imply that he is *not* man, we fall straight into dualism because we are virtually saying that Brahman is not man! If this interpretation is incorrect, I err in good company, for, to quote Woodroffe again,

the *Vishvasara Tantra* says: "What is here, is elsewhere. What is not here, is nowhere." The unseen is the seen, which is not some alien disguise behind which it lurks. Experience of the seen is the experience of the unseen in time and space. The life of the individual is an expression of the same laws which govern the universe. Thus the Hindu knows, from his own daily rest, that the Power which projects the universe rests. His dreamless slumber when only Bliss is known, tells him, in some fashion, of the causal state of universal rest. From the mode of his awakening and other psychological processes he divines the nature of creative thinking. (*Ibid*. p. 36)

The state of infinite formlessness only describes Brahman in His condition of rest (*pralaya*), and it does not follow from this that the enlightened sage, while living in this world, sees all the forms of life as a vain, empty illusion drifting like insubstantial smoke across the face of a void. Such world-denying philosophy does not represent the true meaning of Vedanta, for it is said in the *Isa Upanishad*:

> In darkness are they who worship only the world, but in greater darkness they who worship the infinite alone. He who accepts both saves himself from death by knowledge of the former and attains immortality by the knowledge of the latter.

So much for the doctrine. We now have to see into the state of mind which underlies it, described in the *Mandukya Upanishad* as

> that which is not conscious of the subjective, nor that which is conscious of the objective nor that which is conscious of both, nor that which is simple consciousness, nor that which is a mass all sentiency, nor that which is all darkness. It is unseen, transcendent, unapprehensible, uniferable, unthinkable, indescribable, the sole essence of the consciousness of self, the negative of all illusion, the ever peaceful, all bliss, the One Unit;— this indeed is *atman* (the Self), it should be known.
>
> *Trans.* M. N. Dvivedi.

One has to be careful of these negative descriptions which so delight the Hindu mind and remember the Chinese saying that "between the All and the Void is only a difference of name."[5] For on the one hand the Upanishads say that Brahman is all, while on the other they apply the technique of "*neti, neti*"—"not this, not this"—to show that no individual thing is, as such, a sufficient description of Brahman. Therefore it cannot be said that the knowledge of Brahman is consciousness of the subjective, because this at once excludes consciousness of the objective and all other states of consciousness as well. In regard to these states Brahman is each and all, but none to the exclusion of others. In terms of psychology this is the complete acceptance of all possible states of mind and of all possible circumstances, for to say that all things are Brahman is another way of saying that all things are to be accepted—even non-acceptance, we must add if our non-dualism is to be thorough.

Thus there is nothing man can do to attain union with Brahman, for whether his state of mind is *vidya* (enlightenment) or *avidya* (ignorance) it is nevertheless Brahman. Any attempt to gain that union by *doing*, by making changes, is egoistic pride, being man's attempt to achieve by his own power what already *is* by the power of Brahman. Such pride, to use a popular phrase, is only man's own funeral; it does not affect Brahman. In this very moment all men are Brahman in spite of and because of themselves, and by no possible means can they make or break that union; man can only become conscious of it, not as metaphysical truth but as spiritual freedom, by seeing his own nature as it is and relaxing that contraction (*sankocha*) of egoistic pride which will not let his nature be as it is, and which is forever trying to get away from it by making a virtue of acceptance. Deliverance (*kaivalya*) or freedom is not the result of any course of action, whether mental or physical or moral; according to Vedanta it comes only by Knowledge in the special sense of *gnana* (Gk. γνῶσις) as the fruit of "meditation," which is *being* rather than *doing*.[6]

The Hindu mind was ever in search of "that One thing, knowing which, we shall know all." Obviously, knowledge in this sense is not just factual information; the phrase is another way of saying that the whole cannot be known by the sum of its parts. Thus to know all is not to know about everything, for, as Woodroffe explains, it is not an experience *of* the whole but the experience-whole.[7] This becomes clearer when we understand the reasons for which the experience was originally sought. Our ordinary, partial experience is always limited: joy is conditioned by sorrow, pleasure by pain, life by death, and knowledge by ignorance. Therefore the Hindus conceived freedom as an experience which had no conditioning opposite and called it union with Brahman, the "One-without-a-second." For man is always bound so long as he depends for his happiness on a partial experience; joy must always give way to sorrow, otherwise it can never be known as joy. But the "experience-whole" has no opposite; all the pairs of opposites exist in it, and therefore it may be described as the total acceptance of experience as we know it now, at this and at every moment. There is no greater freedom than the freedom to be what you are *now*. To this experience of freedom the doctrine of Brahman is a key for those who have the wits to use it, for the East does not give out its wisdom in plain statements for all and sundry to use or abuse as they please. It gives hints and makes everyone work hard to unravel their meaning on the principle of "cast not your pearls before swine."

EARLY BUDDHISM

But inevitably there came a time when the experience was obscured by the doctrine, when the psychology of religion became the philosophy of religion and the Brahmanic tradition degenerated into scholasticism, ceremonialism, and fantastic extremes of asceticism whose object was not to accept the opposites but to destroy them, so negatively was the doctrine interpreted. In the depths of this degeneration there appeared in India one Gautama Siddhartha, a prince of the Sakya clan, afterward known as the Buddha, which is perhaps the most tremendous title that a son of India could be given. According to the tradition, Buddhas arise in the human race about once in every five thousand years at times when the "True Law" is forgotten among men. The word "Buddha" is derived from the root *budh*—"to know," and a Buddha is thus one who is supremely enlightened or awakened, one who has plumbed the uttermost mysteries of the universe and attained all knowledge, one who, out of his time, has reached the full height of human evolution. No one can tell whether Gautama was actually such a being, for the imaginative mind of the Orient has undoubtedly added much legend to fact, and it cannot be said that such a giddy height of attainment is the immediate object of subsequent Buddhist thought and practice. As we shall see, in China at least the word "Buddha" has been understood in a more immediately practical sense, although the deepest reverence is still accorded to the supreme Buddhas, to Gautama, Amitabha, and the various Dhyani Buddhas of Mahayanist theology.

Although we have in writing a prodigious number of words attributed to the Buddha, little is known of him. For a long time after his death (*circa* 550 B.C.) his words were passed from mouth to mouth and learned by rote—hence their tabulated mnemonic form—and when they were finally set down in writing their style bore little relation to the spoken words of any human being that ever lived. The earliest records of his teaching are found in the Pali Canon, three large groups of scriptures which read, for a great part, like a statistical report compiled on wet afternoons by monks who had nothing better to do. Another considerable section (the *Vinaya*) contains the very elaborate system of rules and regulations for the conduct of the monastic order (*sangha*), most of which were probably invented in later times and ascribed to the Buddha to give them the necessary sanction. Again they are obviously the work of those whose time was so slightly filled that they could devote hours and hours to the invention of pettifogging restrictions. As for the sections on psychology, never were there such ponderous lists of minutiae, the apparent aim of which is to analyze the human being down to the last detail and so prove that he does not really exist. One has every sympathy with the Chinese Buddhist master who described these records as "lists of ghosts and sheets of paper fit only to wipe the dirt from your skin." The actual, positive teaching has the same tendency to repetitiveness and decomposition, having the general aspect of a flat, barren plain without any definite mountains or valleys; it just goes on and on. It seems nothing less than a miracle that a great world religion can have grown on such a foundation, but I do not think it did.

Here and there we find oases in this desert of words—passages of the same profound beauty which graces the Upanishads and of a somewhat similar meaning. These will be found principally in a collection of sayings known as the *Dhammapada* (of which I recommend the translation by Mrs. C. A. F. Rhys Davids).[8] They are found, too, in some of the *Dialogues* and in other isolated sections of the Canon, and they stand out in such contrast to the rest that they are immediately recognizable as the words of a truly great mind. Therefore to arrive at some idea of the Buddha's teaching we have to take such passages and consider them in their historical context, in relation to what came before them and to what developed out of them. We must remember that the Buddha was active at a time when Hinduism was in a decline, when spiritual experience had been forgotten in its symbols. Except in some few instances his own teaching was swept away in this decline and became so devitalized that it ultimately died out in the land of its birth. But for some hundreds of years a truly vital tradition lived on in India, drawing to it some of the best minds then existing among the Brahmins. This tradition finally came north to China, Tibet, and Japan, and in China Buddhism achieved its full glory in the blending of Indian profundity with the Chinese senses of reality, beauty, and humor.

THE BUDDHISM OF GAUTAMA

The Buddha's teaching is unique in its utter lack of theology; it concentrates wholly on the necessity of arriving at a personal, immediate experience and dispenses with the doctrinal symbol of that experience. In this respect it is the only truly psychological religion. It is a mistake to say that the Buddha denied the existence of any kind of God or soul; these were subjects he simply refused to discuss on the grounds that mere talking and mere belief were not conducive to enlightenment. "One thing do I teach," he said. "*Dukkha* and deliverance from *dukkha*." It is usually translated "Suffering and deliverance from suffering," but for us the word "suffering" is rather too sweeping. I prefer the translation "discord" or even "unhappiness." According to him the cause of discord or unhappiness was *tanha* or selfish craving, which is perhaps best understood as refusal to accept the "three signs of being." These are:

1. *Anicca*—Change or Impermanence.
2. *Anatta*—Literally, "No-self." The unreality of the ego as a permanent, self-contained and self-directing unit.
3. *Dukkha*—In this context, suffering in its widest sense.

THE ONE IN THE MANY

Many people have thought that in making *anatta* one of the three signs of being the Buddha denied absolutely the existence of any eternal principle in man whatsoever. Actually he denied nothing more than the self-existence of the ego (see above, Ch. 1, p. 23), and although as a general rule he refused to discuss the existence of a "Higher Self" (which would be identical with Brahman) there is no doubt that he had it in mind, for he refers directly to it in several places.[9]

When these three signs of being are fully accepted, man attains the experience of Nirvana, whose literal meaning is the dying-out of the fire of *tanha*. In order that no one should confuse doctrine with experience he only described Nirvana negatively and would say nothing positive about it at all. Nirvana, resulting from the acceptance of the three signs of being, is deliverance from *sangsara*, the "Wheel of Birth and Death"—a general symbol of limited experience, of the bondage of the spirit in the wheel of opposites where all that we like is conditioned by what we dislike. Figuratively (and perhaps actually; we do not know) Nirvana is understood as deliverance from the necessity of being reborn again and again in this world of *sangsara*. For *sangsara* is just like what we have called the vicious circle—a circle which turns on and on as long as we try to grapple with the opposites in their own terms, as long as we set pleasure against pain, life against death, permanence against change, and acceptance against escape. The "Wheel of Birth and Death" is indeed the squirrel-cage of man's unhappiness, pursuing himself in order to escape from himself. It is like a bar revolving on its center; the more you push against one end of it, the more it revolves.

Total acceptance of the three signs of being culminates and fulfils itself in the experience of enlightenment or awakening (*bodhi*), which is the abrupt transition from the dual to the non-dual view of life, for Nirvana is sometimes described by the same negative method as employed by the Vedantins in regard to Brahman (cf. the passage quoted above from the *Mandukya Upanishad*). Thus in the Pali Canon alone there is an abundance of evidence to show that Nirvana indicates the same experience of non-duality; a somewhat neglected passage from the Canon puts this beyond all doubt, for Gautama says:[10]

> Thus the Tathagata (Buddha) knows the straight path that leads to a union with Brahma. He knows it as one who has entered the world of Brahma and has been born in it. There can be no doubt in him.

This is one of a few hints that the Buddha's view of life went far deeper than many of his disciples admit. For, after his death, his followers began to separate into two great divisions known subsequently as the Mahayana (Great Vehicle) and Hinayana (Lesser Vehicle). It was as if the seed planted by the Buddha had sprouted into two stems, of which one continued to grow while the other withered. For the Hinayana (now confined to Ceylon, Burma, and Siam) stuck to the letter of the Pali Canon, "working upon it," to borrow an appropriate sentence from Bacon, "as the spider worketh its web, bringing forth cobwebs of learning, admirable for its fineness of thread and work, but of no substance or profit." In their hands the Buddha's teaching decomposed just as their psychology decomposed man and the universe, proving the non-existence of all things.

MAHAYANA BUDDHISM

But the Mahayana began where the Buddha left off—if indeed there is no truth in the claim that Mahayana is the

Buddha's esoteric teaching. It explored further into the psychology of enlightenment, the nature of Nirvana and *sangsara* and the spiritual ideals of Buddhism. One tradition claims that the secret of enlightenment was passed, by a direct mystical communication, down the Mahayana line from patriarch to patriarch of the order.[11] Yet although Mahayana by no means escaped the scholasticism of the Hindu mind, and although, contrary to the Buddha's own practice, it indulged in some of the most subtle metaphysical speculations that man has produced, it established a number of principles which have formed the basis for the greatest spiritual achievements of Buddhism.

The Hinayanists looked upon Nirvana as an escape from the pains of life and death—a conception which to the Mahayanists with their Brahmanic background appeared as the old error of dualism. Thus the ideal man of the Hinayana was the Arhat—one who simply attained Nirvana and ceased from rebirth, entering into the formless rest, bliss, and impersonality of the eternal. But the Mahayanists gave their philosophy of non-duality practical expression in the ideal of the Bodhisattva, who attains liberation but remains in the world of birth and death to assist all other beings to enlightenment. In other words, they refused to make any absolute distinction between Nirvana and *sangsara*; the two states are the same, seen, as it were, from different points of view. Therefore the great *Lankavatara Sutra* says:[12]

False imagination teaches that such things as light and shade, long and short, black and white are different and are to be discriminated; but they are not independent of each other; they are only different aspects of the same thing, they are terms of relation, not of reality. Conditions of existence are not of a mutually exclusive character; in essence things are not two but one. Even Nirvana and Samsara's (*sangsara*) world of life and death are aspects of the same thing, for there is no Nirvana except where is Samsara, and no Samsara except where is Nirvana. All duality is falsely imagined.

Trans. D. T. Suzuki.

In terms of practical psychology this means that there is no actual distinction between our ordinary, everyday experience and the experience of Nirvana or spiritual freedom. But for some people this experience is binding and for others liberating, and the problem is to achieve what the *Lankavatara* calls that "turning about in the deepest seat of consciousness" which effects the transformation.

Now the Mahayana was more thoroughgoing in its statement of this problem than even Vedanta. For what is our ordinary, everyday experience? It is not just our awareness of external circumstances or even such ordinary activities as walking, eating, sleeping, breathing, and speaking; it includes also our thinking and feeling—our ideas, moods, desires, passions, and fears. In its most concrete form ordinary, everyday experience is just how you feel at this moment. In a certain sense Buddhism is very much a philosophy and a psychology of the moment, for if we are asked what life is, and if our answer is to be a practical demonstration and not a theory, we can do no better than point to the moment—*now!* It is in the moment that we find reality and freedom, for acceptance of life is acceptance of the present moment now and at all times. This is not to give the impression that the psychological process is a succession of lightning-quick acts of acceptance, as if they were hurried jabs with a sword that have to be thrust home before the enemy of "making a virtue of acceptance" has spoiled things by carrying us once again into the vicious circle. Acceptance of the moment is allowing the moment to live, which, indeed, is another way of saying that it is to allow life to live, to be what it is now (*yathabhutam*). Thus to allow this moment of experience and all that it contains freedom to be as it is, to come in its own time and to go in its own time, this is to allow the moment, which is what we are *now*, to set us free; it is to realize that life, as expressed in the moment, has always been setting us free from the very beginning, whereas we have chosen to ignore it and tried to achieve that freedom by ourselves.

For this reason Mahayana Buddhism teaches that Nirvana or enlightenment cannot really be *attained*, because the moment we try to attain it by our own power we are using it as an escape from what is now, and we are also forgetting that Nirvana is unattainable in the sense that it already *is*. To quote the *Lankavatara Sutra*:[13]

Those who are suffering or who fear suffering, think of Nirvana as an escape and a recompense. They imagine that Nirvana consists in the future annihilation of the senses and the sense-minds; they are not aware that . . . this life-and-death world and Nirvana are not to be separated.

And again:

Some day each and every one will be influenced by the wisdom and love of the Tathagatas of Transformation (Buddhas appearing in the world) to lay up a stock of merit and ascend the stages (of spiritual achievement). *But, if they only realized it, they are already in the Tathagata's Nirvana, for, in Noble Wisdom* (arya-prajna), *all things are in Nirvana from the beginning.*

Indeed, from beginningless time, Nirvana has been achieved for us and we have only to accept or realize it. It is much the same, psychologically speaking, as the Grace of God in Christianity, but because of our pride we will not recognize it in our experience of this moment and so do not allow ourselves to be free. In the words which Edwin Arnold put into the Buddha's mouth

> Ye suffer from yourselves. None else compels
> None other holds you that ye live and die,
> And whirl upon the wheel, and hug and kiss
> Its spokes of agony,
> Its tire of tears, its nave of nothingness.

Therefore to those who, in this pride, are trying to use enlightenment as an escape from themselves the Mahayana says:

When people attain Enlightenment but still continue to cherish the notion of Enlightenment, it means that Enlightenment itself has become an obstructing delusion; therefore, people should follow the path to Enlightenment until in their thoughts worldly passions and Enlightenment become one thing.

And again in the *Saptasatika*:[14]

Bodhi (Enlightenment) is the five offences, and the five offences are Bodhi. . . . If there is one who regards Bodhi as something attainable, something in which discipline is possible, that one commits self-arrogance.

From one point of view this is dangerous wisdom. There is no better antidote to spiritual pride, but, on the other hand, it might be used as an excuse for any amount of licentiousness. In Buddhism, wisdom is power and sometimes its symbol is a thunderbolt (*dorje*)—a gigantic force that may be used for good or ill. For reasons that will shortly appear, I do not feel that it is a force for ill when rightly understood, but Buddhism took no chances and never neglected to keep in the forefront the Buddha's moral precepts. By themselves these precepts and their observance do not produce that wisdom. But they prepare the ground for it and make man safe for it, disciplining him so that he acquires a taste for morality and becomes less and less likely to use the power of wisdom against his own interests and those of human society. The monastic moral code of Buddhism is perhaps stricter than that of any other religion, and though this code becomes absurd when the secret of that wisdom has been lost, it is tremendously important when the real thing flourishes. Some of us wish that the West would put the same restrictions on the use of the physical powers of science. Sometimes I believe that the Mahayana scriptures were made long and difficult reading so that lazy monks who might try to abuse them would go to sleep in their studies. Even so, there is no doubt that the Hindu mind found a glorious opportunity for subtle hair-splitting in setting out the fine distinctions between Nirvana and *sangsara*, enlightenment and ignorance, for the Mahayana scriptures form the largest bible in the world. The whole Mahayana Canon comprises some sixteen hundred works, some of the longer ones, of which there are an appreciable number, running into as many as a hundred and twenty volumes! Even so, we are told that certain parts of it have been lost.

TAOISM AND THE "I CHING"

In form rather than content the native Chinese religion of Taoism presents a refreshing contrast. It has only four important scriptures, all of which are eminently readable, straightforward, and brief; these are the works of Lao Tzu, Chuang Tzu, Lieh Tzu and Huai-nan Tzu. Its basic principles, however, are so close to those of Buddhism that the two faiths often became blended and were able to improve one another in many ways, especially as to form and method. According to tradition Lao Tzu, the founder of Taoism, was a contemporary of the Buddha and also of Confucius.[15] Although some, after a modern fashion, have denied his existence the story persists that Lao Tzu was a court librarian who, before departing to the western mountains to end his days in retirement, left behind the short collection of sayings known as the *Tao Te Ching*. Chuang Tzu lived some four hundred years later and stands in somewhat the same relation to Lao Tzu as St. Paul to Jesus Christ; his writings are longer and in some ways more developed than Lao Tzu's, one of their chief features being a large supply of anecdotes and parables which are an unending feast of wisdom and humor.

Taoism is based on three fundamental principles, known respectively as *Tao, Te,* and *Wu-wei.* Many attempts have been made to translate the word Tao—the Way, Reason, God, Law, the Logos, Nature, Life, and Meaning. Jung, who worked with the German Orientalist Wilhelm, has called it the principle of *synchronicity* and has also made it mean personality in a special sense of the word.[16] All these terms, however, only give certain aspects of the meaning of Tao, and I prefer to follow the example of those Orientalists who have left it untranslated. The idea of Tao is found in Chinese thought long before the time of Lao Tzu; originally it meant "speech" and thus the *Tao Te Ching* appropriately opens with the pun, "The Tao that can be *tao*-ed is not Tao," or, as Ch'u Ta-kao renders it, "The Tao that can be expressed is not the eternal Tao." In the *I Ching* or *Book of Changes* the "synchronistic" aspect of Tao is uppermost, and this little-understood work must be given some consideration because many authorities hold, and I believe rightly, that the *I Ching* is almost the foundation of Chinese thought. To my own knowledge the word does not occur philosophically in the actual text of the *I Ching*; but it is found in the appendices, of later date, and there is no doubt at all that the Chinese concept of Tao has been greatly influenced by the *I Ching*. Moreover, the "synchronistic" aspect of Tao has contributed largely to the Buddhist psychology of the *moment*.

The *I Ching* is probably the second earliest of the great Chinese classics, and according to Legge was written in 1143 B.C. or thereabouts. It is generally used as a book of divination, but probably has much profounder uses. "If some years were added to my life," said Confucius, "I would give fifty to the study of the *I*, and might then escape falling into great errors."[17] The actual text is an analysis of sixty-four hexagrams made up of eight trigrams, sets of divided and undivided lines corresponding to the eight principal factors or elements of life. One of these hexagrams (made up of two of the trigrams) is said to show the two main factors involved in any situation at a particular moment. The divided lines show the principle of *yin* (negative and female) and the undivided lines that of *yang* (positive and male), the two aspects under which Tao operates in the world of form. (*See diagram.*) The *I Ching* and the system of divination based upon it has, I believe, puzzled so many Westerners because it presupposes a view of life and a way of reasoning which are quite foreign to us. This is what Jung terms the principle of *synchronicity*.

All our reasoning is based on the law of cause and effect operating as a *sequence*. Something is happening *now* be-

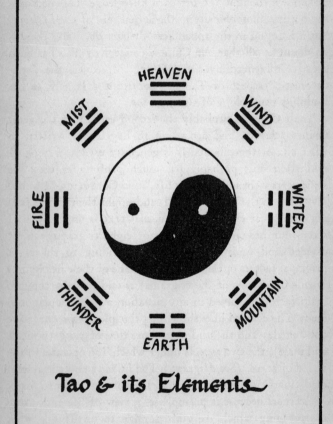

Tao & its Elements

cause something else happened *then*. But the Chinese do not reason so much along this horizontal line from past, through present to future; they reason perpendicularly, from what is in one place now to what is in another place now. In other words, they do not ask why, or from what past causes, a certain set of things is happening now; they ask, "What is the *meaning* of those things happening together at this moment?" The word Tao is the answer to this question. The present situation within and around oneself is Tao, for the present moment is life. Our memory of the past is contained in it as well as the potentiality of the future. In short, this way of looking at things is based on a great appreciation of the significance of the moment, and implies that all things happening now have a definite relation to one another just because they have occurred together in time, if for no other reason. This is another way of saying that there is a harmony called Tao which blends all events in each moment of the universe into a perfect chord. The whole situation in and around you at this instant is a harmony with which you have to find your own union if you are to be in accord with Tao. When you have discovered your own union with it, you will be in the state of Te, sometimes rendered as "virtue" or "grace" or "power," but best understood as Tao realized in man. Of this Lao Tzu says in his laconic style, "High Te is not Te and thus has Te; low Te does not lose Te and thus is not Te," which Ch'u Ta-kao renders, "The superior virtue is not conscious of itself as virtue; therefore it has virtue. The inferior virtue never lets off virtue; therefore it has no virtue."

Tao and Te are best understood by considering the principle which joins them, which makes Tao appear in man as Te. This is *wu-wei*, the secret of harmony with Tao in its spiritual aspect. Other and slightly different orders of *wu-wei* give harmony with the Tao in its material aspects, and it is with these that the *I Ching* is primarily concerned—with the conduct of everyday affairs, politics, strategy, economics. For while the *I Ching* explores the mechanics, the parts and the detailed relationships of the momentary harmony, the purpose of Taoist psychology is to feel it as a whole; the former is analytic and the latter synthetic. Literally *wu-wei* means "non-doing" or "non-assertion" and is often mistranslated as "doing nothing." But *wu-wei* means "non-doing" simply in the sense that by no *action* of our own can we bring ourselves into harmony with Tao, for, as we have seen, the secret of this harmony-in-the-moment is not action but acceptance of a harmony already achieved by Tao itself. We do not alter the actual situation; but our attitude toward it undergoes a change whereby we feel harmony where before we felt discord. This change Chuang Tzu illustrates by the story of "Three in the Morning."[18]

A keeper of monkeys said with regard to their rations of chestnuts, that each monkey was to have three in the morning and four at night. But at this the monkeys were very angry, so the keeper said that they might have four in the morning and three at night, with which arrangement they were all well pleased. The actual number of the chestnuts remained the same, but there was an adaptation to the likes and dislikes of those concerned.

Trans. Giles.

Wu-wei as acceptance indicates that the only difficulty of Taoism is its unheard-of simplicity. Thus Lao Tzu says:

My words are very easy to know, and very easy to practice.
Yet all men in the world do not know them, nor do they practice them.

The reason for this simplicity is given in the third appendix of the *I Ching*. In the fifth chapter Legge's translation reads:

> The successive movement of the inactive (*yin*) and active (*yang*) operations constitutes what is called the course of things (Tao). That which ensues as a result of their movement is goodness; that which shows it in its completeness is the natures of men and things. The benevolent see it and call it benevolence. The wise see it and call it wisdom. *The common people, acting daily according to it, yet have no knowledge of it.* Thus it is that the course of things, as seen by the superior man, is seen by few. (The italics are mine.)

The terms are different, but here is the principal meeting point of Taoism and Mahayana, for, as we read in the *Lankavatara*, "If they only realized it, they are already in the Tathagata's Nirvana, for, in Noble Wisdom, all things are in Nirvana from the beginning." Or, as the Christian says, if you will accept the Grace of God, you are saved as you are. The principle seems an outrage on common sense, backed by the egoism of moral ambition, and in a very complicated universe it seems much too simple, much too ludicrous to be true. Yet, says Lao Tzu,

> When the superior scholar is told of Tao
> He works hard to practise it.
> When the middling scholar is told of Tao,
> It seems that sometimes he keeps it and sometimes he loses it.
> When the inferior scholar is told of Tao,
> He laughs aloud at it.
> *If it were not laughed at, it would not be sufficient to be Tao.*

Zen Buddhism in China

The differences between Taoism on the one hand and Vedanta and Buddhism on the other probably arise from the difference of climate in China and India. The idea of Tao is rather more dynamic than that of Brahman; Tao is the ever moving, momentary course of things, while Brahman is the eternal and the unchanging. The Hindu is leisurely and, like tropical vegetation, his mind is prolix, whereas the Chinese are rather less leisurely, for their land is none too fruitful and in their thoughts they are correspondingly brief and to the point. They rebelled against the wordiness of Hindu Buddhism and also against its tendency to seek wisdom in withdrawal from the world and in lofty states of consciousness without any relation to practical life. For the Hindus did not always follow the teachings of Mahayana to their logical conclusion, and it took Chinese good sense to practice what the profundity of the Hindu mind had conceived. Therefore toward the end of the eighth century A.D. the Chinese had evolved a form of Buddhism which combined all the virtues of Buddhism and Taoism, and, I cannot feel by mere chance, the rise of this Chinese school of Buddhism coincided with the golden age of Chinese culture in the dynasties of T'ang, Sung, and Yuan. In Chinese this school was known as Ch'an, but in the West it is more generally known by its Japanese name of Zen, and it has been summed up as

A direct transmission (of Enlightenment) outside the scriptures;
No dependence on words and letters;
Direct pointing to the soul of man;
Seeing into one's own nature and attaining Buddhahood.

For the founders of the Zen school believed, and rightly, that the secret of enlightenment can never be conveyed in any form of words or contained in any system of ideas. Non-duality or total acceptance defies all intellectual description, being a condition of the spirit having no opposite with which it may be contrasted and so understood. "Enlightenment," according to a Zen teacher, "is your everyday thought"—and yet, what is it that makes the difference between an ordinary man and a Buddha? In accordance with the Taoist feeling for the moment, they called Zen the sudden as distinct from the gradual school of Buddhism, for its object is to see into one's own nature at this moment and so realize that one's own nature is "Buddha-nature." As Tao-wu said, "If you want to see it, see into it directly; but when you stop to think about it, it is altogether missed." Zen as a technique is designed to solve the following problem: how, without resorting to the confusion of intellectualism, are we to demonstrate the oneness of Nirvana and *sangsara*, of Tao and life, and of spiritual freedom and everyday experience? If we say in so many words that Tao is what you are experiencing at this moment, this is no more than a concept. Furthermore, whenever we say that this or that *is* Tao, we are still speaking in terms of dualism; we are joining two things together that were never in need of joining, and still keeping in the back of our minds the distinction between "this" on the one hand and "Tao" on the other. In other words, the idea of Tao, Buddha, Nirvana, Brahman, or whatever it may be, is only confusing while it remains an idea, a concept over, above, and apart from ordinary experience. So how can we demonstrate Tao as a reality instead of a concept? How can we point to life and show man that it is Tao and that it can set him free without calling it by that name? After all, Tao and Nirvana are only names for an experience; those who invented them had the experience first and gave it its name afterwards, but now people are so busy learning about the names that they forget the experience.

method of teaching evolved by the Zen masters was therefore a kind of spiritual "shock-tactics" designed to demonstrate the experience itself in so concrete and forceful a manner that the disciple would be brought to a sudden realization. We have already recounted the somewhat unusual method used by Hui-neng to awaken the thief who tried to steal his robe and bowl, but his successors resorted to even more unusual tactics. The following examples have been rendered by Dr. D. T. Suzuki from early Chinese sources.

Zen master Bokuju was once asked, "We have to dress and eat every day, and how can we escape from all that?" The master replied, "We dress; we eat." "I do not understand." "If you do not understand, put on your dress and eat your food."

When Gensha was treating an officer to tea the latter asked, "What does it mean when they say that in spite of our having it every day we do not know it?" Gensha took up a piece of cake and offered it to him. After eating the cake, the officer repeated the question, thinking the master had not heard him, whereat Gensha replied, "Only that we do not know it even when we are using it every day."

On another occasion a disciple asked Gensha how to enter the Path. Said Gensha, "Do you hear the murmuring of the stream?" "Yes, I do." "*There* is a way to enter."

A Confucian scholar came to Kwaido to ask about Zen. Kwaido answered, "There is a passage in the text you are so thoroughly familiar with, which fitly describes the teaching of Zen. Did not Confucius declare, 'Do you think I am holding something back from you, Oh my disciples? Indeed, I have held nothing back from you.'" The scholar could not understand this, but later when they were walking together in the mountains they passed a bush of wild laurel. "Do you smell it?" asked Kwaido. When the scholar answered that he did, Kwaido exclaimed, "There, I have kept nothing back from you!"

What are these men trying to convey? Does Kwaido wish to show the scholar that the scent of wild laurel is Tao or Nirvana? Indeed no! If that had been Kwaido's idea, he would have said it in so many words. He just wanted the scholar to experience the scent of wild laurel. These stories are rather like jokes. The moment you try to explain a joke it falls flat, and you only laugh when you see the point directly. Thus to explain these stories is really to explain them away. Now Zen never explains; it only gives hints, for, as van der Leeuw has said, "The mystery of life is not a problem to be solved, but a reality to be experienced." Trying to explain Zen is like trying to catch wind in a box; the moment you shut the lid it ceases to be wind and in time becomes stagnant air. For "the wind bloweth where it listeth, and thou hearest the voice thereof but canst not tell whence it cometh nor whither it goeth. Even so is everyone that is born of the Spirit."

THE BARRIER OF THE OPEN ROAD

Some have thought that Zen is just a kind of "naturalism," and so it would seem to be if we were to take, say, the following from Rinzai at its face value:[19]

You must not be artful. Be your ordinary self. Seeking in the external world, if you would fain find your hands and feet by inquiring of your neighbors, you are committing an error. If you seek after Buddha, Buddha will turn out to be just a mere name. Rather know him who seeks for Buddha. . . . You yourself as you are—that is the Buddha Dharma (Law). I stand or I sit; I array myself or I eat; I sleep when I am fatigued. The ignoramus will deride me but the wise man will understand. . . . If you master any place where you are, that place becomes true ground. . . . Therefore the ancients said that if you make an attempt to acquire the law, the law will not operate naturally and all the evil circumstances will push their heads up competitively. When the sword of wisdom comes forth, there will be nothing at all— no enticement of any sort in the world. Then you will see the bright half of darkness in the darkness itself, and will see also the dark half of brightness in brightness itself. Wherefore the ancients said that the everyday mind is the true law.

Trans. Sokei-an Sasaki.

In one sense this may be naturalism, but no one was ever natural who *tried* to be natural nor even anyone who tried not to try. As soon as we set up a technique of trying, we miss Rinzai's meaning, for Zen is no sort of cult or "ism," and the moment we make it into one we fall straight into the vicious circle. But Rinzai's meaning is "clear as the vastness of the sky," though to see it we have to see it directly, as if it were a joke. Again and again he admonishes his disciples to see themselves as they are at this moment, for "what you are making use of at this moment, is just what makes a Buddha."

More than the old Mahayana, more even than Taoism, Zen concentrates on the importance of seeing into one's own nature now at this moment—not in five minutes when you have had time to "accept" yourself, nor ten years ahead when you have had time to retire to the mountains and meditate. The Zen masters resort to every possible means to direct your attention to yourself, your experience, your state of consciousness as it is now, for, as we have said before, there is no greater freedom than freedom to be what you are now. In our pride we are loath to accept freedom from an experience so apparently humble and prosaic. But there is another factor in the Zen realization. For as soon as you allow yourself that freedom, you realize that, after all, it is not a question of *allowing*; you see that there was never a time when you did not have that freedom. When understood, the full acceptance of what you are now, of your present state of mind, whatever its nature, shows you that you have been making that full acceptance all along, though you never knew it; it shows you that whatever your experience may have been in the past and whatever it will be in the future, nothing in yourself or in the whole universe has deprived or can ever deprive you of that freedom. Before this realization you seem to be confronted by a barrier standing across the path and dividing the road of freedom from the road of bondage; but as you pass through that barrier it vanishes, for it never existed and the whole road was free.

There is a Zen book called the No-Gate-Barrier (*Mu-mon-kwan*) which Nyogen Senzaki translates as "The Gateless Gate."[20] Its author introduces it with this verse:

> No gate stands on the public road.
> Those who pass this barrier
> Walk freely throughout the universe.

A master was once asked by his disciple, "Pray show me the way to deliverance." The master replied, "Who has ever put you in bondage?" "Nobody." "If so," concluded the master, "why should you ask for deliverance?" Another, when asked the same question, answered simply, "Where do you stand now?" Yet another, who was asked a question to the same effect, replied, "There are no by-roads, no crossroads here; the hills all the year round are fresh and green; east or west, in whichever direction, you may have a fine walk." This is indeed straight talking, so clear that it is hard to see, but we shall always think we are blind while we go round looking for sight with open eyes. On one occasion the great master Ummon said:

"In Zen there is absolute freedom; sometimes it negates and at other times it affirms; it does either way at pleasure." A monk asked, "How does it negate?" "With the passing of winter there cometh spring." "What happens when spring cometh?" "Carrying a staff across his shoulders, let him ramble about in the fields, east or west, north or south, and beat the old stumps to his heart's content."

Joshu said, "The Great Way is right before your eye, but difficult to see." A monk asked, "What form does it take so that we can see it before us?" "To the south of the river or to the north of it, just as you please."

The literature of Zen is full of such instances, but the Catholic sinologue Wieger could see in it no more than "a collection of folios filled with incoherent, crazy answers. . . . These are not, as one might have supposed, allusions to esoteric matters which one would have to know in order to understand. They are mere exclamations escaping from the mouths of morons, momentarily awakened from their coma."[21] Needless to say, the accomplished master of Zen is hardly ever found in anything remotely resembling a coma except when he sleeps at night, and although they occasionally refer to themselves as morons Zen masters have been responsible for some of the most superb works of art that China and Japan have produced. It is difficult to see how Wieger could have missed the feeling of freedom in so many of these sayings; for in the man who carries a staff across his shoulders and rambles in the fields, east or west, north or south, beating the old stumps to his heart's content, do we not find the same state of soul as in the wind that "bloweth where it listeth" and which is likened to everyone that is born of the Spirit?

His thatched cottage gate is closed, and even the wisest know him not. No glimpses of his inner life are to be caught; for he goes on his own way without following the steps of the ancient sages. . . . He is found in company with wine-bibbers and butchers; he and they are all converted into Buddhas.

Kakuan.[22]

Perhaps one of the best ways to catch a glimpse of the Zen experience of freedom is to read its poetry. Thus Hokoji says:

> How wondrous and how miraculous, this—
> I draw water and I carry fuel.

Then we have this from Mumon:

> Hundreds of spring flowers; the autumnal moon;
> A refreshing summer breeze; winter snow:
> Free thy mind of idle thoughts,
> And for thee how enjoyable is every season!

The free man walks straight ahead; he has no hesitations and never looks behind, for he knows that there is nothing in the future and nothing in the past that can shake his freedom. Freedom does not *belong* to him; it is no more his property than the wind, and as he does not possess it he is not possessed by it. And because he never looks behind his actions are said to leave no trace, like the passage of a bird through the air.

> Bamboo shadows sweep the stairs
> But stir no dust;
> Moonlight reaches the depths
> But leaves no trace in the pool.

Here is the verse of one who has suddenly seen the truth and goes forward into life a free man:

> For this one rare event
> Gladly would I give ten thousand coins of gold!
> With a hat on my head and a bundle at my side,
> On my staff I carry the breeze and the full moon!

There was one who became enlightened at the sudden playing of a flute, whereat he wrote these lines:

> In the days when I had no insight
> My heart was sad at the playing of the flute;
> But now I have no idle dream—
> I let the flute-man play on as he wills.

Do not mistake these poems for the sentimental feelings of untrammeled nature-lovers, living far from cities and modern drudgery. The surface of sentiment covers thunder and lightning. Here is the reaction of a Zen poet in the face of sudden death:

> Neither earth nor heaven give me refuge;
> Body and soul melt to nothingness.
> Your sword, a lightning-flash,
> Cuts like the wind of spring!

Yet another in the same strain runs:

> Under the sword raised high
> Is hell. In fear your tremble,
> But walk on!—
> And there is the Land of Bliss.

In Zen we discover the central truth of Oriental wisdom standing naked and unashamed—shorn of its trappings and symbols. At times it seems utterly perplexing and again utterly absurd. But it does not differ from the supreme experience which lies at the heart of every other faith aiming at freedom of the spirit. Yet we are so used to symbols and doctrines, so cluttered up with the mere images of wisdom which the ages have handed down, with the names of the God whose Self remains unseen, that when someone points directly to the experience itself we are taken aback and cannot believe our eyes. This is the more so when that which is pointed out is something lying right under our noses and which ordinarily we are too proud to consider. But God is always found where He is least expected, and no one would have thought of looking for Him in the cowshed of a country inn.

And if Zen reveals to us the central experience of Oriental religion, no one can say that Asia can offer us only the *via negativa* of denying the world. Eastern philosophy makes an illusion of man and the universe only as a step to making them divine, so that we may see a wonder and a miracle in the drawing of water and the carrying of fuel. For in the doctrine that each creature and thing is a transitory aspect of the eternal Brahman only a benighted mind could read a denial of living forms; yet the intention was to accord them the most tremendous affirmation that man could utter.

Those who search for happiness do not find it because they do not understand that the object of their search is the seeker. We say that they are happy who have "found themselves" for the secret of happiness lies in the ancient saying, "Become what you are." We must speak in paradox because we think we are divided from life and, to be happy, must unite ourselves with it. But we are already united, and all our doings are its doings. Life lives us; we do not live life. Yet in fact there is no "us" apart from life that life can so "live." It is not that we are passive tools of life, as fatalists believe, for we could only be passive tools if we were something other than life. When you imagine yourself to be divided from and at war with life, you imagine yourself to be its passive tool and so are unhappy, feeling with Omar Khayyám—

> Oh, Thou, who Man of baser Earth didst make,
> And who with Eden didst devize the Snake;
> For all the Sin wherewith the Face of Man
> Is blacken'd, Man's Forgiveness give—and take!

But in truth action and passivity are one and the same act, and life and yourself are one and the same being. This truth of ancient philosophy is beyond our logic, but he who understands it is a sage and he who does not is a fool. But, curiously enough, the fool becomes a sage by letting himself be free to be a fool; then his joy knows no bounds and he "walks freely throughout the universe." One might call this the complexity of the very simple. And this, without the use of technical terms, is the answer of Oriental wisdom to the toughest problem of Western thought—the problem of fate and free will.

FATE AND FREE WILL

Inevitably, the search for spiritual freedom brings us to this time-honored conundrum. For, it will be asked, is not the total acceptance of life as we have described it simply the most thoroughgoing fatalism? Does it not mean just the huge sense of irresponsibility which arises from the knowledge that not only your deeds and circumstances, but also your very thoughts and feelings, are the acts of life or fate—and you may as well cease to be worried by them? If this is true, does it not also imply that those who persist in the apparent bondage and very real misery of refusal to accept, believing in free will and taking pride in their ego-istic powers, are in fact unable to experience that accept-ance, fate having decreed their belief in free will? When Oriental philosophy says that all things are Brahman, Western intellectualism cannot resist applying the label of fatalism. The reason is that we have not been able to resolve the problem of the vicious circle, for determinism or fatalism is its philosophic description. The vicious circle is the impotence of man; it is not resolved until the realiza-tion of our impotence as men can be complemented by our omnipotence as God. This is the point where fatalism bursts into freedom. Curiously enough, few philosophers have ever dared to be consistent fatalists because the doctrine contains an odd paradox. Fatalism is the doctrine of man's utter subservience to destiny, but one strange objection is always raised to it—"If everyone believed that all their thoughts and deeds were inevitably foreordained by fate, *then people would behave just exactly as they pleased.*" In other words, they would become dangerously *free*!

Total acceptance as we have described it is very nearly this carrying of fatalism to the point where it becomes absolute liberty. But it contains an additional factor which guards the process against its dangers and makes it something much more than a mere proposition in philosophy. But first we must consider the problem of fatalism in its purely philosophical sense. Logically, the position of the fatalists is unassailable; they reason that a given cause can have only one effect and that there can be no activity of the human mind which is not the effect of a cause. Thus whenever a choice of actions is presented to us, our decision is determined not by a free act of will but by the untold number of factors which make up our being at that moment—hereditary impulses, instinctive reflexes, moral upbringing, and a thousand other tendencies which incline us to a particular choice as inevitably as a magnet draws a needle lying within its field. An act of choice could not be free unless it were done without motive, for our motives are the result of past conditioning. But motive is only another name for cause, and an action without any kind of cause is impossible. Thus we have a chain of cause and effect, in which each cause is an effect and each effect a cause; each link in this chain can only have two particular links on either side of it, before as cause and after as effect. Therefore the last link in the chain is predetermined by the first.

With Earth's first Clay They did the Last Man's knead,
And then of the Last Harvest sow'd the Seed:
  Yea, the first Morning of Creation wrote
What the Last Dawn of Reckoning shall read.

THE FREEDOM OF FATE

Yet, strictly speaking, this amounts in the end to a proof of free will, but a more tremendous free will than the advocates of that doctrine ever contemplated. For if each one of our acts is determined by the entire previous history of the universe, if sun, moon, planets, and stars are at work in the winking of an eyelid, this means that we in our turn are *using* their power in all our doings. For the doctrine of fatalism, from one point of view, amounts almost to God's giving man *carte blanche* to use His power in whatever way He pleases. Objectively it may be true that in a determined universe fatalism gives you anything but the power to do as you please, but purely objective matters have little or no direct meaning for human beings when it comes to the really important things of life, and it is a truism that cold facts have no meaning apart from that which we give to them. As a rule, fatalists are those who try to understand life in terms of strictly rational and objective values. ("Objective values" have probably as much reality as cubic colors.) But if determinism is a cold fact its meaning depends entirely on the subjective attitude we take toward it, and it is seldom that the rationalist has either the courage to accept its power to liberate or sufficiently abject pessimism to take the other attitude and say with Andreyev

I curse the day on which I was born. I curse the day on which I shall die. I curse the whole of my life. I fling everything back at your cruel face, senseless Fate! Be accursed, be forever accursed!

With my curses I conquer you. What else can you do to me? . . .
With my last thought I will shout into your asinine ears: Be accursed, be accursed!

But even on the objective plane it does not follow that
determinism deprives us of all freedom, because no Western
metaphysician or scientist has yet decided what is the precise
difference between the soul of man and fate itself.

Now Oriental philosophy is quite clear on this point,
and for this reason has never found any stumbling-block in
the fate-freewill problem. Vedanta says that the soul of
man is Brahman, which means that our own deepest self is
that First Cause which set the wheels of fate in motion.
But then Vedanta does not share our common-sense view
of time, for only from the standpoint of *maya* was the First
Cause a thing of the past. In reality the First Cause is forever *now*. We speak of the beginning and the end of the
universe in terms of aeons, kalpas, and ages simply because
human intellect cannot grasp the nature of eternity unless
it is spread out upon the measuring-rod of time. But to
the Oriental philosopher the creation and destruction of
the universe are taking place in this moment, and for him
this is true from both the metaphysical and the psychological standpoints. It is not our purpose to enter into the
former because it is quite outside everyday experience, and
has no more to give to the solution of immediate human
problems than the scientific or objective view.

In terms of practical psychology I would say that this
metaphysical concept of the East is a state of mind in which
the relation between oneself and life, fate, or destiny is no
longer a question of moved and mover, passive agent and
active power. Therefore it involves a change from the view
of life in which man is an isolated being without any sense

of union or positive relationship between himself and the rest of the universe as it exists both externally and within the soul. Spiritual freedom is not apparent in this state because man as an isolated unit has no meaning, just as the finger is meaningless without the hand, and the hand without the whole body. A life without meaning is unhappiness, and we have this lack of meaning whenever man's view of life is not whole, whenever man sees himself as a creature whose desires and whose very human nature have no positive relation to the universe.

In this view we are the merest whims of fate who can only find salvation in letting ourselves drift on the sea of chaos or in fighting for everything that we can hold. Man can never understand his freedom while he regards himself as the mere instrument of fate or while he limits his freedom to whatever his ego can do to snatch from life the prizes which it desires. To be free man must see himself and life as a whole, not as active power and passive instrument but as two aspects of a single activity. Between those two aspects there may be harmony or conflict, but conflict itself may also proceed from that single activity. Thus man's experience becomes whole when he sees the activity of life as a whole in himself as he is now, when he realizes that there is no difference between his own thoughts and actions as they are at this moment and the nature of the universe. It is not that life is making him think and move as you pull the strings of a marionette; it is rather that man's thoughts and deeds are at once his own creations and the creations of impersonal nature. Man's volition and nature's activity are two names for one and the same thing, for the doings of life are the doings of man, and the doings of man are the doings of life.

Two as One

Here there is no question of which is the mover and which the moved, for man lives his life by the same power with which life lives man. This is why total acceptance, which seems to be a response to bondage, is actually a key to freedom, for when you accept what you are now you become free to be what you are now, and this is why the fool becomes a sage when he lets himself be free to be a fool. Indeed, we are always free to be what we are now and only false pride keeps us from seeing it. Therefore acceptance is activity and passivity in one; as passivity it is accepting ourselves, our desires, and fears as movements of life, nature, and the unconscious; as activity it is letting ourselves be free to be ourselves and to have our desires and fears. Whereupon the ego and the unconscious, man and nature, oneself and life are seen as the two dancers who move in such close accord that it is impossible to say which moves and which responds, which is the active partner and which the passive. It is possible to have this feeling of wholeness not only in rare moments of insight but also in everyday living, and this comes just as soon as we realize that all our activities are just as much activities of nature and the universe as are the circling of planets, the running of water, the roaring of thunder, and the blowing of the wind.

In this understanding we shall move forward as freely and uninterruptedly as the wind. But our freedom will not inflate us if we see that we share it will all things under the sun; for if you think you can possess and acquire freedom it will inflate you to the point of bursting with spiritual pride. Therefore it is not a question of putting yourself artificially into a certain state of mind, for freedom is no different from the state of mind you have now, and whether you realize it or remain ignorant it makes no difference to your freedom. But we are always trying to interfere with our states of mind as they appear from moment to moment, imagining that some are nearer to freedom than others— singing "Nearer my God to Thee" instead of "Just as I am, Thou wilt receive." This very interference drives out the sense of freedom, for spiritual pride is to imagine that some creatures and some states of mind are nearer to God than others. Now acceptance becomes love when it enables us to see that God does not depart from us even when we are sinful men.

But does man have freedom only through God? In other words, can he realize his freedom only in the moment when he is predestined to do so and not before? This question has been much of a puzzle to the theologians, the Calvinists having taken the view of predestination and the Catholics, generally speaking, the view that although man is not free to be good without the Grace of God, he is nevertheless free at all times to choose the acceptance of Grace. Thus Berdyaev writes in his *Freedom and the Spirit*:

If human nature was definitively perverted and the freedom of the spirit definitively impaired, there would be no faculty in man capable of receiving the truth of revelation and he would be insensible to the operations of grace. But man though wounded and broken remains a spiritual being and has preserved his religious consciousness, for the Word of God could not be addressed to a being who was deprived of it. Liberty in man precedes the action of revelation and grace. (pp. 130-131.)

The answer seems confused because the question is wrongly stated. Both the Calvinist and the Catholic answer seem to fall short of the mark through not recognizing that man's acceptance of Grace is one and the same act as God's giving of it. Man's free choice does not *precede* the action of Grace, nor does it *follow* it, and it cannot be said that the initiative comes from either side. The two acts occur simultaneously because they are two aspects of the same process; man's ascent to God is God's descent to man. The theologians are confused because they make too hard and fast a distinction between God and man—a distinction which, in view of the Christ symbol, the God-man, they should have avoided. As St. Athanasius said, "He became man that we might be made God."[1] Therefore, in Christian terms, the descent of God into man as Christ is a historical symbol of an eternal event—a union of God and man in which neither ceases to exist (for Christ was as much man as God) and a union which achieves realization from both sides at once. Eckhart puts it in this way:

It is as if one stood before a high mountain and cried, "Art thou there?" The echo comes back, "Art thou there?" If one cries, "Come out!" the echo answers, "Come out!"

The echo only *follows* the call because there is physical space between man and mountain, and because the mountain has no tongue and cannot call and be echoed by the man. But God and man have a closer union, and Eckhart says that "the eye with which I see God is the same with which God sees me."[2] Realization is not predestined to come at a certain time because predestination is an utterly limited half-truth. It may come at any moment, for that union exists eternally. Fate is only the other face of freedom, and we may say that you are fated to realize it at a certain time only because you choose to see it at that time.

This argument will not, of course, appeal to those who

argue fatalism on the basis of causality in the objective universe. These will argue that although fatalism may perhaps give one a wholly imaginary sense of freedom, events will nevertheless occur only in their predestined time and thus the development of a sense of freedom will be as fated as anything else. This type of fatalism takes no account of the possible relationships between the self of man and the "cause of Fate" and depends to a great extent on the common-sense view of time. Factual knowledge of these matters is rudimentary, to say the least, and hence we cannot regard the argument as in any way final. Moreover, the psychology of the unconscious argues against the lesser type of free will (i.e., the usual theological notion) on different grounds, explaining the apparently free decisions of the conscious ego as "rationalizations" of unconscious impulses. But here it parts company with the argument from causality, for many psychologists of this school do not admit that causality applies within the unconscious.[3] From the spiritual standpoint, however, the purely philosophic and scientific arguments are irrelevant; such metaphysical premises as it employs may be regarded as "working hypotheses"; the important thing is that they should be "*working.*" Scientist and philosopher may argue to the end of time, but meanwhile the human soul thirsts, and psychologist, priest, and mystic have the temerity to suggest that there may be ways of approach to the ultimate mysteries other than laboratory observation and pure logic. For while scientist and logician dissect and analyze, the mystic looks for meaning in the whole.

At each moment the mystic accepts the whole of his experience, including himself as he is, his circumstances as they are, and the relationship between them as it is.

Wholeness is his keyword; his acceptance is total, and he excludes no part of his experience, however unsavory it may be. And in this he discovers that wholeness is holiness, and that holiness is another name for acceptability. He is a holy man because he has accepted the whole of himself and thus made holy what he was, is, and shall be in every moment of his life. He knows that in each of those moments he is united with God, and that whether he is saint or sinner the intensity of that union never changes. For God is the wholeness of life, which includes every possible aspect of man and is known in accepting the whole of our experience at each moment. And for those who do not understand the word God, I quote from Goethe's *Fragment upon Nature*:

Nature! We are encompassed by her, enfolded by her—impossible to escape from her and impossible to come nearer to her. . . . The most unnatural also is nature. Who sees her not on all sides sees her truly nowhere. . . . At each moment she starts upon a long, long journey and at each moment reaches her end. . . . She lets every child enlarge upon her, every fool judge her, thousands pass heedlessly over her, seeing nothing; yet she has friends among all and has her recompense from all. Even in resisting her laws one obeys them; and one works with her even in desiring to work against her. . . . Love is her crown. Only through love does one come near her. . . . She has isolated all things so that she may bring all together. . . . All is eternally present in her, for she knows neither past nor future. For her the present is eternity.

FREEDOM AND LIBERTINISM

Indeed, Goethe's words seem to suggest a freedom of terrifying possibilities, possibilities which the sages of Asia have known and understood, and which the mystics of Christianity may also have known but of which they have spoken only with the greatest care. For all things are possible to the free man—*but not probable*. His freedom is founded in the knowledge that his union with God, life, or nature can never be destroyed; that while he lives (and perhaps when he is dead) he can never do anything but express God or nature in all that he thinks and does. He is free because he knows that even if he descends to the uttermost depths of depravity he can in no way deny or separate himself from a universe which includes all extremes and hence can suffer from none. For as God "maketh his sun to rise on the evil and the good" so also He provides them with that of which His sun is a symbol—Himself. As Whitman says in his poem "To a Common Prostitute,"

Not till the sun excludes you do I exclude you,
Not till the waters refuse to glisten for you and the leaves to
rustle for you, do my words refuse to glisten and rustle
for you.

Thus in the freedom of the spirit we understand that whether we love life or loathe it, whether we are filled with compassion or hatred, wonder or lust, beauty or horror, wisdom or ignorance—each and all of these opposites are as acceptable as day and night, calm and storm, waking and sleeping. We do not feel bound through any preconceived pattern of good character to react to our experience in the "proper" way; at any moment we may react to that experience just exactly as we please and consciously be just as uninhibited as the wild animal is by instinct. In sorrow the free man feels himself free to weep, in pain to scream, in anger to kill, in tedium to get drunk, and in laziness to idle. It is precisely this feeling of freedom which absolves him from the necessity of doing these things, and there is another reason too of which we shall speak later. He is like a man with a fire-hose; the nozzle is his physical body and

brain, and the water is the power of life. He is free to turn
that hose in any conceivable direction, for by no twist or
turn can he cut off the supply of life-giving water which
never ceases to flow out in all its power. In moods of depression or sluggishness we may think that it has run low, but
this is only because we do not give the mood freedom to
expand itself; we are pointing the nozzle at the ground and
the force we employ to keep it down is our effort to repress
the mood.[4]

THE DANCE AND THE CENTER

We have a popular phrase that describes this freedom—
"Let yourself go!" In the language of religion and psychology it is called self-abandonment. Essentially self-abandonment to life is a knack. A deliberate attempt to abandon
oneself cannot be done without faith, for it seems like
taking a plunge into a roaring torrent. Confucius tells of
a man who managed to come safely down a huge water-
fall by abandoning himself to the nature of falling water.
But faith will follow abandonment provided we do not
hang about on the brink and prevent ourselves from jump-
ing by an increasing rush of misgivings—provided we jump
immediately. This is to abandon yourself to your experience, your state of mind as it is at this very moment, being
prepared to let it take you wherever it wills. But, as we have
seen, as soon as you let life live you, you discover that you
are living life with an altogether new fullness and zest. To
return to the analogy of the dance, it is as if you allowed
your partner, life, to swing you along until you so get the
"feel" of the dance that you are doing the "swinging" just
as much as your partner. And then she will laugh at you
and tell you that you were doing it all the time, only that

you were so busy trying to figure out the steps by yourself that you forgot your partner and even forgot that it was a dance.

Thus the free man has the feeling of an unchanging center in himself—a center which is not exactly in his ego and not exactly in life, nature, or the unconscious as independent of the ego. It is the middle of the dance, the point around which the two partners revolve and in which they realize union. He is free because this center makes him feel absolutely secure and at home in the universe; he can take it anywhere, make it do anything, for, as Lao Tzu says of the Tao, "Using it, he finds it inexhaustible." This center is the point on which his feeling of wholeness depends, and it develops out of faith—because he trusts and abandons himself to life on the one hand and to himself on the other, and also to the dance that is between them. God imparts His life and strength to all creatures, trusting them to use it as they will, because God is the principle of faith and love. When man can have that same faith and love for all the creatures of his mind, which are the states of his mind from moment to moment, then he becomes at one with God. Indeed, the kingdom of heaven is within us—microcosm of the macrocosm—and man finds his freedom through faith in his own universe, making the sun of his acceptance to rise on the evil and the good. Now in this there is profound humility, for as God knows Himself in the sinner as well as in the saint, in the slime as well as in the stars, so also man, in partaking of the freedom of God, must recognize himself in his depths as well as in his heights. For our true instructors in wisdom are not the sages and their writings but the creatures of our own minds, the gods and demons of thought and feeling and their reactions to the outer world of experience. And of these demons the blackest of all is called Lucifer, the bearer of light, for he is made to show us that there is light in the darkness as well as in the light. In the words of Monoimus the Gnostic:[5]

Cease to seek after God (as without thee), and the universe, and things similar to these; seek Him from out of thyself, . . . and learn whence is sorrow and joy, and love and hate, and waking though one would not, and sleeping though one would not, and getting angry though one would not, and falling in love though one would not. And if thou shouldst closely investigate these things, thou wilt find Him in thyself, one and many, just as the atom; thus finding from thyself a way out of thyself.

Man's life begins when he awakens to his freedom, and the earlier in life he discovers it, the better for him. Religion in this sense is not the goal of life; it is the entrance to it, and in freedom of the spirit man has the most glorious instrument of creation that he could desire. For he has discovered God not only in thoughts *about* God but also in thought itself, and knows himself to be thinking God even when his attention is absorbed in worldly affairs. To those affairs he brings a new power, zest, and spontaneity, for he can give himself to them unreservedly in the knowledge that spirituality is by no means confined to thinking about "spiritual" things. Thus he can devote himself to thoughts of people and things, of business, music, art, and literature, of science, medicine, and engineering, of eating and drinking, of walking, breathing, and talking, of swimming, running and playing, of looking at the stars and of washing his hands; he has the freedom of God because he is free to think of everything and anything. For if it is true that the innumerable objects of the universe are the thoughts of God, this is what God Himself is doing. Now if his realization of freedom is genuine, it will have two important results—one of which will follow in its own time, and another which, coming immediately, will safeguard him against the abuses of freedom.

THE FULFILLMENT OF PERSONALITY

Those who realize their freedom early in life will probably not experience the first result until after the age of forty or some years, always provided that they do not allow the instrument of freedom to become rusty; it has to be cleaned and sharpened like any other tool. But there will ultimately come a time when this freedom will effect a change in their psychological structure which will be noticeable in their dreams and fantasies. For just as constant playing of the piano alters the structure of the hands, constant freedom alters the structure of the psyche. This change comes about gradually, whereas freedom itself is usually realized suddenly; but the psyche must then adapt its "organs" by slow growth to the use of its newly found instrument. When the psyche is fully adapted to its freedom we have the condition which Jung describes as "individuation"—a *consequence* and not a cause of spiritual freedom. The main features of this condition have already been described (see Ch. 4, pp. 90-93), but certain aspects of it must be clarified. We spoke of freedom as the feeling of a center in one's being, an unchanging point of balance which can enter into all circumstances without loss of stability. At first this center is "ideal" in the Platonic sense, and may be compared to the idea of a tune in the composer's mind before it has been played on an instrument or set down on paper. But because it is ideal, it is none the less real; it is not *an* ideal in the sense of a mere wish for the future. When the composer thinks, "One day I shall compose a most glorious symphony," he may be said to have *an* ideal. But when every note of it is heard in his mind and only remains to be given the vehicle of mechanical sound, it is then in the ideal state. To the composer, however, that symphony is very real and its beauty may possibly have a profound effect on his life. So also the ideal center of freedom may have a profound effect on one's life, even before the faculties of the psyche are adapted to give it the fullest possible expression.

In fact, however, I would set no limits to the possibilities of expressing spiritual freedom, and a hundred lives would not be long enough to exhaust them. But just as music demands four voices for the full expression of melody and harmony, so the human being demands four fully grown faculties to express the complete possibilities of freedom—and even so they are still expressing only *possibilities*. Jung classifies the four faculties or functions of man as intuition, sensation, intellect, and feeling, and it is almost impossible that anyone should be awakened to all of them before the middle of life.[1] These four form a cross with intuition opposite sensation and intellect opposite feeling, and as a rule we grow up and reach the middle of life with only two unopposed faculties developed. Thus, to return to the analogy of music, we can express freedom only with the treble and alto voices; we may *feel* the center of the cross, but not be aware of all its arms. These two voices or faculties may express the freedom perfectly well within their limits, but the composer will want to express his feeling more completely. Therefore in time we are able to add the more mature voice of tenor and ultimately reach the fully mature voice of bass. It is as if the four petals of a flower had opened one at a time; when all are open, it remains for the flower to grow. So, when the composer has expressed all four voices in solo instruments, he will begin to add to them so that string quartet becomes chamber orchestra and ultimately full-sized symphony orchestra. Or we may take the musical analogy in another way and liken the four faculties to the four orchestral divisions—strings, wood-wind, brass, and percussion.

We do not, however, achieve this fourfold development simply by seeking out the four individual parts. The petals of a flower grow from the center and the raison d'être of the orchestra is the symphony, and of the four voices, the tune. Spiritual freedom, therefore, gives us the consciousness of a center upon which and out of which these four facul-ties can grow, though the center is not fully a center until all four are equally developed. The center of a semicircle is only *ideally* the center of a circle. Therefore in youth we may achieve that center of freedom, but the psyche which hinges upon it will be somewhat lopsided and immature. With astonishing persistence the symbols of this fourfold development occur in religion and mythology the world over. In Christianity it is the Cross, in Buddhism the swastika, the fourfold *mandala* and the crossed *dorje* round a circle, in early Chinese philosophy the four *hsiang* or em-blems of the *I Ching*, in playing-cards the four suits—the list might be elaborated indefinitely.[2]

In later life this fourfold development may be consciously evolved, though many fail to realize it because they are unaware of their freedom and so have no creative center. They merely succumb to the spells of the unconscious, for-getting the reality of freedom in its psychological symbols. For the symbols of individuation which appear in dreams and fantasies grow as vehicles for freedom and follow the actual "pattern" of freedom. They may grow even if freedom is unrealized—just as some people have brains but no minds—but it is usual that in such cases the dream-pictures show the four faculties with an empty or undeveloped center. But Jung describes the center as a "virtual point *between* the ego and the unconscious" because, as we have seen, freedom arises from *total* acceptance. That acceptance is not just the one-sided act of the ego "letting go" to life or the unconscious and so denying completely its egoistic nature. This is a false dualism. Total acceptance includes both the ego and the unconscious, pays due regard to the demands of both and unites them without destroying their functional difference. Therefore in the process of individuation the psyche may be said to grow a new "organ" which Jung calls the self as distinct from the ego on the one hand, and the unconscious on the other. This self, as the vehicle of freedom, appears as a rule only in the ripeness of years when freedom has become a habit and has shaped the human organism to suit its ends, just as perpetually running water carves out a permanent course in the rock. This is the fulfillment of personality.

The Opposites as an Expression of Love

But in some ways even more important is the immediate result of a genuine realization of freedom. This is that response of the individual to God known as worship or adoration, having its foundation in love. In the understanding of our freedom we learn that however low we may sink, we can never separate ourselves from the power of life and the love of God. For in learning to accept all possible states of our own souls, we learn that God accepts all possible types of human being, animal, and devil. The physical symbol of this love is the sun, though, like all physical symbols, it is incomplete. Although the physical universe visits us with both joy and pain, life and death, in the spiritual realm all these opposites are reconciled. Not only are they mutually necessary to one another, but, taken together, life and death constitute a more glorious life than life alone—a truth which can only be proved in acceptance. For if we can learn to love both life and death, we find that life and death are in turn an expression of love. If we can learn to love, to accord freedom to both the heights and the depths of our own nature, we shall instantly realize that this love is not something that we have produced alone but is in the very nature of the universe, and that our heights and depths are unintelligible without it. Just as love is the meaning of man and woman and has its symbol in the child, so only love can explain all other opposites under the sun. And this meaning, this love which is the raison d'être of opposites exists long before our acceptance of the opposites reveals it, for acceptance is only a way of seeing that which already exists. Without these many opposites there could no more be a universe than there could be melody without the sounding and silencing of notes, and only those who do not accept them can complain that the universe was unfortunately arranged. Unaccepted, the universe has no meaning; it is senseless fate and chaos, but acceptance is a way of discovering meaning, not of manufacturing it.

Thus there are heights and depths in man just as there is day and night in the external world, and both are seen as manifestations of the love of God when man himself learns to love them, for the love of God and acceptance by man are two aspects of one and the same reality. In the words of Eckhart, "As God can only be seen by His own light, so He can only be loved by His own love."[3] Love, however, is not to be confused with liking; we may love the opposites, but because of our human nature we cannot always like them. Only the pervert actually *likes* suffering, but the love of suffering is known in giving freedom to your dislike of it; for without dislike on our part, suffering is no longer suffering.[4]

THE GRATEFUL RENUNCIATION

The revelation through acceptance that in love we are free as to both our heights and our depths, calls out from us a response of love and wonder for life and for God, if we can see life as the outer aspect of God. We remember the words of St. Augustine, "Love, and do as you will," for in love, as in acceptance, man denies no aspect of his nature. He realizes that life or God has given him freedom to be everything and anything that is in him, whether good or evil. But, as Eckhart says, "there is no inner freedom which does not manifest itself in works of love."[5] For the free man is so filled with gratitude to life for the freedom to be all of himself *that he joyfully renounces it*. This is where true freedom guards itself against abuse. Gratitude makes it possible to sacrifice the freedom to be immoral in the realization that immorality and sin are petty and tedious. In a universe where freedom of the spirit offers such gigantic possibilities, sin is a simple waste of time. To use a commonplace analogy, it is like gorging oneself with saccharine when one might be eating a skillfully prepared banquet. For in the last analysis sin is bad taste; it is sensationalism as distinct from sensibility.

Because of his gratitude the free man's religion is principally a means of saying, "Thank you." It is no longer a means of discovering salvation, for religion as a quest for personal illumination is necessary but selfish, and until freedom is discovered it is a blind attempt to create for oneself what is simply to be had for the taking—"searching for fire with a lighted lantern." Thus the religion of freedom consists of using that freedom and giving thanks for it, because it is only a dead faith that does not show itself in works. At the same time freedom is a tremendous responsibility. There is a saying that though God forgives you, nature never forgives, for the free man does not escape in any way from the material consequences of folly. If he abuses his freedom he does not lose it, but he has to pay the material price for abuse—a price which is greater for him than for others. It is as if his thoughts and deeds were informed with a greater power and thus produced more powerful results. All men use the power of God, but those who use it in full consciousness have to be particularly careful how they use it. It is difficult to believe, however, that anything but a radical misunderstanding of freedom could lead to abuse, so great is the gratitude which arises from true understanding.

As a rule this gratitude demands expression in the ritual of worship, for some rituals were originally a dance of joy. As Christ is made to sing in the apocryphal *Acts of John*:[6]

> Grace danceth. I would pipe; dance ye all.
>
> .   .   .   .   .
>
> The Whole on high hath part in our dancing.
> Whoso danceth not, knoweth not what cometh to pass.

At times the free man conducts his ritual of thanksgiving silently within himself; at other times he conducts it in churches and temples with other people, giving it every possible embellishment of music, song, and visual beauty. As a religion Buddhism started without a God, but the principle of "Buddha" had to be raised to the level of God simply to offer a focal point for the gratitude which the experience of freedom or Nirvana inspired. It is therefore significant that Zen, philosophically and practically a destroyer of forms and images, has quite an elaborate temple ritual. Although it insists, perhaps more than any other form of Buddhism, on the inwardness of the Buddha principle, nevertheless the physical images of the Buddhas are treated with the greatest reverence. Iconoclasm may be necessary for bringing about the realization of freedom, but thereafter we find a new feeling for all religious symbols of life, of the universe, and of that "Love which moves the sun and other stars."

But there are those whom symbols can never satisfy, and moreover the gratitude of freedom is so overflowing that the forms of religion can never absorb it. This gratitude therefore demands expression in "works of love," which is to say morality. It makes possible for the first time a genuine morality, for the free man is moral because he *wants* to be, not because he thinks he *ought* to be moral. Without gratitude morality is a mere discipline which keeps human society in a relatively stable condition until such time as men learn the freedom of love. But as a discipline it cannot teach love, and as a religious exercise it is no more than imitation of the free man's behavior. Freedom as liberty to be all of oneself is amoral, but the gratitude which comes in response to this liberty is moral. Freedom is like a gem which shines with equal brilliance in all surroundings; it gleams as well in mud as on velvet, but those who appreciate it do not let it lie in the mud and so arrange the conduct of their lives that the gem is given the most exquisite setting that can be made. But just as precious stones have to be dug out of the depths of the earth, so man has to realize his freedom in accepting the earthy depths of his own being.

Realization has done its work when one's very life becomes an expression of gratitude, and this is the greatest happiness, for the meaning of happiness consists in three elements—freedom, gratitude, and the sense of wonder. These three elements can be present in the most ordinary of lives; the free man is not necessarily a magician, a seer or a "mystic" absorbed in ineffable states of consciousness. So many people make the mistake of looking in the super-sensual realms for the happiness which they cannot find here on earth, searching for an occult "cosmic consciousness" to release them from the tedious experiences of every-day life. It can never be said too often that the Great Illumination is not a fantastic, extraordinary state of consciousness remote from normal experience. It is every conceivable state of consciousness and of unconsciousness as well (though in unconsciousness it cannot be seen), but people are misled by the symbolic forms in which it is expressed. The Great Illumination is the state of consciousness you have at this moment, and it is recognized as such only when you cease to run away from it and give it freedom to reveal itself. And having found freedom in so unexpected a place, you will be filled with gratitude and then with wonder. For in its greatest form wonder is reverence for all the forms of life, from the highest to the lowest; it is an appreciation of the mystery that divinity is revealed in the most commonplace of things. For this reason Dmitrije Mitrinovic (a too-little-known philosopher of Yugoslavia) once said that *gnosis* was to be surprised at everything.

THE EXPERIENCE OF MYSTERY

As a rule vast knowledge of the mysteries of the universe increases pride, and to lay bare all mysteries is to be in danger of becoming bored. If you try to discover the secret of beauty by taking a flower to pieces, you will arrive at the somewhat unsatisfactory conclusion of having abolished the flower. For beauty is beauty just because it is a mystery, and when ordinary life is known as a profound mystery then we are somewhere near to wisdom. Here is a new connection between mystery and mysticism, a connection which is sometimes indignantly denied. But are we to cast aside all scientific curiosity and embrace the maxim that where ignorance is bliss 'tis folly to be wise? Of course, the catch is that every degree of wisdom has its counterpart in folly, and the two are so alike that the wise man is wise simply because he can distinguish between the two. The highest and lowest notes of musical sound are both inaudible, and the ignoramus and the sage are both faced with mystery. The difference between the two is that even if you explained the mystery to the sage, it would still remain mysterious, whereas the fool would simply be disappointed and disillusioned. For the fool would imagine that the explanation, the taking to pieces, the analysis, had spoiled the mystery; the sage would see that it had not even begun to explain it. The fool would think he had thereby become wise; the sage would know that he was still a fool. Therefore if the sage is told, as some "mystics" will tell him, that this everyday world is a mere phantom conjured up by deceptive senses from a formless primordial essence, he is not much impressed. If a doctor explains the transformations undergone by food in his stomach, he does not cease to enjoy his dinner. If a scientist tells him that thunder is not the music of the gods but mere electrical disturbances, the thunder is for him no less wonderful. And if some Philistine tells him that playing a violin is only scraping cats' entrails with horsehair, he simply marvels that melody can emerge from things so unprepossessing in appearance. For what is especially interesting about explanations is that they do not explain; and what is especially dangerous about them is that if they are taken seriously enough and far enough, they simply explain things away. And even if one does resort to the ultimate madness of explaining all things away, there remains still the impenetrable mystery of who is it that explains and why?

"L'Amor Che Move . . ."

Thus to the free man there is as much divinity and mystery in a brick as in all the ramifications of occult science, for to him a brick is a magic. There is as much freedom of the spirit in watching sparrows on a city street as in meditating in some mountain solitude under the stars. There is as much expression of that freedom in peeling potatoes as in making a cathedral organ sing out the liquid thunder of a fugue. For the free man has become aware of the mystery that the whole power of the universe is at work in the least of things, the least of thoughts, and the least of deeds. In lifting his finger he uses the same power that hurls the stars through space and causes their fire, that bellows in thunder and whispers in wind, that produces a giant tree from the microscopic germ of a seed, and wears away mountains to thin clouds of dust. In whatever he feels, thinks, or does he cannot cut himself off from that power; he knows that in spite of all mistakes, imaginings, and fears he can never for a moment cease to share in its tremendous freedom. He knows that he expresses it both in living and in dying, in creating and in destroying, in being wise and in being a fool. Even so he is not inflated with the conceit of himself as a spiritual giant who has accepted all life and reconciled all opposites. He knows that because of the love of God life was never in need of being accepted nor the opposites of being reconciled, for in acceptance he has only awakened to see what that love has achieved from the very beginning of time. Worms, fleas, idiots, and drunkards are in fact accepting it as much as he, and even though they do not know it as he knows it, he cannot deny them a particle of the reverence that is given to saints and sages. He sees that if anyone is a fool it is himself for not having discovered his treasure long before. Thus in the moment of illumination he realizes that the universe is a mystery greater than he can ever hope to fathom, for the deepest perplexity of all is that such a creature as himself should be allowed to use the power that moves the stars in the littlest of his deeds. Whereat he will say with Dante,[7]

> Ma non eran da ciò le proprie penne,
>   se non che la mia mente fu percossa
>   da un fulgore, in che sua voglia venne.
> All'alta fantasia qui mancò possa;
>   ma già volgeva il mio disiro e il velle,
>   sì come rota ch'egualmente è mossa,
> L'amor che move il sole e l'altre stelle.

> (But my own wings were not for such a flight—
>   except that, smiting through the mind of me,
>   there came fulfilment in a flash of light.
> Here vigor failed the lofty fantasy;
>   but my volition now, and my desires,
>   were moved like wheel revolving evenly
> By Love that moves the sun and starry fires.)

NOTES

INTRODUCTION

[1] *The Secret of the Golden Flower*, Wilhelm and Jung (New York and London, 1931), p. 83.

[2] Here and throughout, the word "life" should not be understood simply in its biological sense, as the vital force which imparts movement to organic bodies. Nor should it be understood as a force which pervades things and moves them while remaining essentially different from them. I use the commonplace word because for many people it has more concrete meaning than the word God. It should be understood in the same sense as the Chinese word *Tao*. William McDougall once asked a Chinese exactly what he meant by Tao. The Chinese took him out to the balcony and asked, "What do you see?" "I see a street and houses and people walking and street-cars passing." "What more?" "There is a hill." "What more?" "Trees." "What more?" "The wind is blowing." The Chinese extended his arms and exclaimed, "That is Tao!" In other words, life is the whole universe as it is now. In this sense the universe should not be considered as just the *sum* of all things, but as a whole which is greater than the sum of its parts. That is to say, the universe or life is an organic unity from which all individual things derive their meaning and to which they must be referred if they are to be understood. For individual things can have neither existence nor meaning if they are unrelated. See the section on Taoism in Ch. 6, and cf. my *Legacy of Asia* (Chicago, 1938), pp. 72-75.

[3] *Mu-mon-kwan*, vii. I am indebted for this translation to the Rev. Sokei-an Sasaki. (See note 19, Ch. 6.)

CHAPTER ONE

[1] Brahman as the Self is not quite the same as the usual concept of a World Soul, for Brahman is not the soul of the universe

as opposed to its body or physical form and substance. Brahman is rather the wholeness of the universe from which all its parts are derived, and which indeed *is* each single part. See the section on Vedanta in Ch. 6.

[2] See his *South American Meditations*, Ch. 2.

[3] Luke 15: 11-32.

[4] Cf. Gooch and Laski, *English Democratic Ideas in the Seventeenth Century* (New York, 1927).

[5] Psychoanalysts have never claimed that the unconscious is anything more than a working hypothesis. They have not insisted on its existence as a particular entity in either the bodily or mental aspects of man. But as a hypothesis it has proved of such value in psychological healing that it seems to matter little whether there is in fact *an unconscious* or not. It is probable that the unconscious would be described more correctly as a process than as an entity, i.e., the process of not being aware of certain operations, tendencies, and impulses that belong to our nature, revealing themselves in indirect or rationalized forms, or not at all.

[6] Jung does not admit that he is a mystic, for he is at pains, and rightly, to emphasize the strictly scientific method of his inquiry—in so far as psychological or any other kind of healing can be a science. For his view of the unconscious see *Two Essays on Analytical Psychology* (New York, 1928), p. 94 *et seq.* Also *The Integration of Personality* (New York, 1939), Ch. 1.

[7] *Maya* is often translated incorrectly as "illusion"—a purely negative rendering which does not give the full meaning. *Maya* is the creative power of Brahman.

[8] *From Fetish to God in Ancient Egypt*, E. A. Wallis Budge (London, 1934), p. 15.

[9] I follow the translation by H. A. Giles in his *Chuang Tzu* (Shanghai, 1926), p. 282.

[10] An interesting study of some of these figures will be found in Rom Landau's *God Is My Adventure* (New York, 1936).

[11] Patanjali's *Yogasutra*, 2, vi.

CHAPTER TWO

[1] A remarkable analysis of this confusion is the first chapter of Nicolas Berdyaev's *Freedom and the Spirit* (London, 1935), esp.

p. 15. "Spirit," he writes, "is by no means opposed to flesh; rather, flesh is the incarnation and symbol of spirit."

² A refreshingly different interpretation of this doctrine will be found in Berdyaev, *ibid.*, pp. 40-41.

³ Psalm 139: 7-12.

⁴ *Mu-mon-kwan*, xxvi.

⁵ See Zimmer, *Kunstform und Yoga* (Berlin, 1926).

CHAPTER THREE

¹ Chapter 5, p. 182. The whole of this chapter is particularly suggestive.

² Romans 7: 5-9.

³ Interpretation of the Bible on these points is not easy because of an inconsistent use of words. Note the apparent contradiction: "For God so *loved* the world . . ." (John 3: 16) and "If any man *love* the world, the love of the Father is not in him" (1 John 2: 15). The Greek ἀγάπη is used in both instances.

⁴ Cf. Friedrich Spiegelberg's *Religion of Non-Religion* (London, 1938), pp. 14-16.

⁵ Tathata is usually translated as "Suchness" (Suzuki). Some people might prefer "Reality," though "Suchness" is rather more demonstrative if less euphonious.

⁶ Trans. Juan Mascaro, *Himalayas of the Soul, Translations from the Sanskrit of the Principal Upanishads* (London and New York, 1938), p. 89.

⁷ See below, Ch. 8.

⁸ *Ibid.*, p. 183.

⁹ For a fuller development of this theme see my *Legacy of Asia* (Chicago, 1938).

¹⁰ For a much fuller treatment of this subject see Jung's commentary to *The Secret of the Golden Flower*, Wilhelm and Jung (London and New York, 1931).

¹¹ *Meister Eckhart's Sermons*, trans. Claud Field (London, n.d.), pp. 19-20.

¹² See *Asiatic Mythology*, J. Hackin and others (London, 1932), facing p. 434. The actual painting is in the Musée Guimet.

¹³ Theurgia or the Egyptian Mysteries, Iamblichos, *trans.* Alexander Wilder (London and New York, 1911), p. 35.

¹⁴ Cf. *Secret of the Golden Flower*, pp. 90-91.

CHAPTER FOUR

[1] See Jung's *Integration of Personality*, Ch. 3, "Archetypes of the Unconscious." For the mana-personality, see *Two Essays on Analytical Psychology*, p. 252 *et seq.* A more popular account will be found in Frances G. Wickes' *Inner World of Man* (New York, 1938).

[2] Cf. Sigmund Freud, *Leonardo da Vinci.*

[3] See G. R. Heyer, *The Organism of the Mind* (London, 1933); H. Prinzhorn, *Psychotherapie* (Leipzig, 1930); J. A. Hadfield, *Psychology and Morals* (London, 1936); E. Graham Howe, *I and Me* (London, 1935) and *War Dance* (London, 1937); Beatrice Hinkle, *The Recreating of the Individual* (New York, 1923). The Pastoral Psychologists, who have now formed an organization in London known as the Guild of Pastoral Psychology, are chiefly interested in promoting an understanding of psychotherapy among ministers of religion. To date they have done some particularly valuable work, including the publication of the following papers: H. Westmann, *The Old Testament and Analytical Psychology*; James Kirsch, *The Religious Aspect of the Unconscious*; W. H. Peacey, *Pastoral Psychology and the Gospel*; C. G. Jung, *The Symbolic Life* (for private circulation only). Their headquarters are at St. George's Institute, Broadbent Street, London, W. 1.

[4] Detailed descriptions of the individuation process will be found in Jung's *Two Essays on Analytical Psychology* and more particularly in *The Integration of Personality.*

[5] Oriental *mandala* are chiefly of Buddhist origin, being widely used by Lamaist Buddhism and the Shingon sect in Japan. Examples will be found in Zimmer's *Kunstform und Yoga*, in the Musée Guimet publication *Asiatic Mythology*, in Oberlin and Matsuo's *Sectes Bouddhiques Japonaises*, pp. 111-112 and in Waddell's *Buddhism of Tibet.* Western *mandala* were much used by the alchemists, and several examples will be found in Manley Hall's *Encyclopedic Outline of Masonic, Hermetic, Qabbalistic and Rosicrucian Symbolical Philosophy* (San Francisco, 1928). More modern *mandala* drawn by Western people will be found in Wilhelm and Jung's *Secret of the Golden Flower*, in F. G.

Wickes' *Inner World of Man*, and in Heyer's *Organism of the Mind*, and in Jung's *Integration of Personality*.

[6] See Hearn's *Glimpses of Unfamiliar Japan*, Vol. II, Ch. 9.

[7] *The Secret of the Golden Flower* (text).

[8] Cf. Jung's essay on this question in his *Modern Man in Search of a Soul* (New York and London, 1933).

[9] See D. T. Suzuki's *Manual of Zen Buddhism* (Kyoto, 1935), also his *Essays in Zen Buddhism*, Vol. I (London and Kyoto, 1927).

[10] For further observations on the individuation process, see below, Ch. 8.

[11] From Ch. 1 of the *Tan-ching* or "Platform Sutra"—the life and teachings of Hui-neng (also spelled Wei-lang), the sixth patriarch of the Ch'an or Zen school of Buddhism in China. Translations are: *Sutra of the Sixth Patriarch*, by Wong Mow Lam (Shanghai, 1930), an edited version of which is to be found in Dwight Goddard's *Buddhist Bible*, 2nd ed. (Thetford, Vt., 1938). Cf. also *Mu-mon-kwan*, xxiii.

[12] See Jung's *Modern Man in Search of a Soul*, Ch. 5, "The Stages of Life." Cf. also my *Legacy of Asia*, pp. 28-29.

[13] *Le Kama Soutra de Vatsyayana*, trans. Isidore Liseux (Paris, 1885). An English version is *The Kama Sutra of Vatsyayana*, Hindu Kama Sastra Society (Benares, 1883).

[14] The following excerpts from the *Tao Te Ching* are from the translation by Ch'u Ta-kao (London, 1937). This same translation appears in its entirety in Ballou's *Bible of the World* (New York, 1939).

[15] See Suzuki's essay "Ignorance and World Fellowship" in *Faiths and Fellowship*, ed. D. A. Millard (London, 1936), p. 40.

CHAPTER FIVE

[1] Cf. Goethe in his *Fragment on Nature*, "She is frivolity itself, but not for us, who have been made to see her as of the greatest importance."

[2] Job 38: 7.

[3] Freedom through abandonment is man's sharing the nature of God. Cf. Berdyaev, "The world is the symbol of that which

transpires within the spiritual sphere, the reflection of God's 'abandon' as fulfilled in the spirit." *Freedom and the Spirit*, p. 33.

[4] A fascinating study of this infinite regression as a psychological problem is Graham Howe's *War Dance, A Study in the Psychology of War* (London, 1937).

[5] Cf. Suzuki in *Faiths and Fellowship*, p. 41. Here he describes *sunyata* or "no-thing-ness" (a Buddhist description of the Absolute) as *byodo* (unity) in *shabetsu* (diversity). He says, "The discrete and yet continuous state of existence is described by Buddhist philosophers as '*Byodo in Shabetsu* and *Shabetsu in Byodo*.'"

[6] Cf. James' *Varieties of Religious Experience* (New York and London, 1929), pp. 205-216.

[7] Cf. Plotinus, "that which mind, when it turns back, thinks before it thinks itself."

[8] Matthew 6: 27-30.

[9] It is important to distinguish between the Jewish and the Hebraic traditions. Post-captivity Judaism suffered much loss of spirit from its slavery to the letter of the law, but this slavery is not to be found in the major prophets such as the second Isaiah. In Christ's time Judaism had captured the priesthood of Jerusalem completely, and the Hebrews of the older tradition were despised.

CHAPTER SIX

[1] The following excerpts are from Juan Mascaro's *Himalayas of the Soul, Translations from the Sanskrit of the Principal Upanishads* (London and New York, 1938).

[2] Cf. Deussen's *Outline of the Vedanta* (London and New York, 1907). "This soul in each one of us is not a part of Brahman nor an emanation from him, but it is, fully and entirely, the eternal and indivisible Brahman itself." p. 1.

[3] *Vita e Dottrina*, p. 36, also cap. xiv. See too Evelyn Underhill's *Mysticism* (London, 1930), pp. 129 and 396.

[4] *Shakti and Shakta*, Sir John Woodroffe (Madras and London, 1929).

[5] *Secret of the Golden Flower* (text).

[6] Cf. René Guenon's *Man and His Becoming According to the Vedanta* (London, 1928), pp. 232-235. With regard to "medi-

tation" in the sense used here, an interesting quotation is found in the *Chandogya Upanishad*, 7, vi: "Meditation is in truth higher than thought. The earth seems to rest in silent meditation: and the waters and the mountains and the sky and the heavens seem all to be in meditation."

[7] *Shakti and Shakta*, p. 28 *et seq.*

[8] In recent years Mrs. Rhys Davids has set herself the difficult task of separating the gold from the dross in the Pali Canon. On the whole her work has been remarkably successful, although there are some occasions when her reasoning seems a little wishful. No one, however, has been able to offer any satisfactory refutation of her claims. Her scholarship is most thorough and I recommend study of her *Outlines of Buddhism* (London, 1934), and her *Manual of Buddhism* (London, 1932), as well as all recent works including revisions of books published before 1918. A short comprehensive survey of this aspect of her work is *What Was the Original Gospel in Buddhism?* (London, 1938).

[9] See *The Book of the Gradual Sayings*, III, trans. E. M. Hare (London, 1934). There is a particularly interesting passage on p. 237. A Brahmin says to the Exalted One, "This is my avowal, this my view: There is no self-agency; no other-agency." The Buddha replies, "Never, Brahmin, have I seen or heard of such an avowal, such a view. Pray, how can one step onwards, how can one step back, yet say: There is no self-agency; no other-agency?" Cf. also *Gradual Sayings*, I: "Thou scorn'st the noble self, thinking to hide the evil self in thee from self who witnessed it." The Self of the Upanishads is often described as the Witness or the Spectator. Another passage from the *Maha-Parinibbana Sutta* is worth considering: "Live ye as they who have the self as a lamp, a refuge."

[10] *Tevigga Sutta*, 43. See *Buddhist Suttas*, trans. T. W. Rhys Davids, Vol. XI of the Sacred Books of the East (Oxford UP, 1900), p. 186.

[11] See Suzuki's *Essays in Zen Buddhism*, Vol. I, Ch. 4.

[12] *The Lankavatara Sutra*, trans. D. T. Suzuki (London, 1932). An edited version of this translation is in Dwight Goddard's *Buddhist Bible* in the second edition of which the passage quoted will be found on p. 292.

NOTES

[13] See Goddard's *Buddhist Bible*, pp. 352 and 356.

[14] *Saptasatika-prajnaparamita Sutra*, 232-234. A remarkably suggestive quotation from this sutra will be found in Suzuki's *Essays in Zen Buddhism*, Vol. II, pp. 251-252n.

[15] But see Arthur Walley's *Way and Its Power* (London, 1935), p. 101 *et seq.*, also pp. 86 and 99. He gives the date of the *Tao Te Ching* as *c.* 240 B.C., and believes that it only became connected with Lao Tzu at a later date.

[16] See *Secret of the Golden Flower*, p. 142, also *Integration of Personality*, p. 305.

[17] *Analects*, 7. xvi.

[18] *Chuang Tzu*, 2.

[19] Unfortunately there is no published translation of the *Rinzai Roku* (Ch. *Lin-chi Lu*), but I am most indebted to Sokei-an Sasaki, Abbot of Jofuku-in, for the loan of an unfinished translation of the work which will ultimately appear in book form.

[20] *The Gateless Gate*, trans. Nyogen Senzaki and Saladin Reps (Los Angeles, 1934).

[21] See Wieger's *Histoire des Croyances religieuses en Chine*, pp. 517-528.

[22] This passage is from Suzuki's rendering of the commentary to the last of the "Ten Oxherding Pictures." See his *Manual of Zen*, p. 161.

CHAPTER SEVEN

[1] *De Incarnatione*, Verbi, 1, cviii.

[2] *Meister Eckhart's Sermons*, p. 32. The whole passage reads: "If my eye is to discern color, it must itself be free from all color. The eye with which I see God is the same with which God sees me. My eye and God's eye is one eye, and one sight, and one knowledge, and one love."

[3] Cf. Fritz Wittels' *Freud and his Time* (New York, 1931), pp. 133-134.

[4] Cf. the following from the *Saptasatika*: "O Sariputra, to commit the offences is to achieve the inconceivable, to achieve the inconceivable is to produce Reality. And Reality is non-dual. Those beings endowed with the inconceivables can go neither to the heavens, nor to the evil paths, nor to Nirvana. . . . Both the

offences and the inconceivables are of Reality, and Reality is by nature non-dual. . . . In the real Dharmadhatu (Realm of the Law) there is nothing good or bad, nothing high or low, nothing prior or posterior." *Trans.* Suzuki.

[5] *Fragments of a Faith Forgotten*, G. R. S. Mead (London, 1931), p. 223.

CHAPTER EIGHT

[1] For a full account of the four functions see Jung's *Psychological Types* (London, 1923; New York, 1933), esp. Ch. 10, sec. 11.

[2] Cf. Jung's *Psychology and Religion* (New Haven, 1938), Ch. 3. Also his *Integration of Personality*, Chs. 2 and 4.

[3] *Meister Eckhart's Sermons*, p. 57.

[4] Cf. *Acts of John*, 96. "If thou hadst known how to suffer, thou wouldest have been able not to suffer. Learn thou how to suffer, and thou shalt be able not to suffer." The translation is by M. R. James in his *Apocryphal New Testament* (Oxford UP, 1924), p. 254.

[5] *Ibid.*, p. 54.

[6] *Acts of John*, 95.

[7] *Paradiso*, 33, cxxxix-cxlv. The translation is by Melville B. Anderson in his *Divine Comedy of Dante Alighieri*, copyright 1921 by the World Book Company, Yonkers, New York.

BIBLIOGRAPHY

THE following bibliography is not intended to be in any way exhaustive, nor does it list all the works consulted in writing this book. It has been made up of easily available works which are likely to be of interest to the general reader who wishes to explore further into the main points raised in this book.

THE PSYCHOLOGY OF THE UNCONSCIOUS

COSTER, GERALDINE. *Yoga and Western Psychology*. Oxford University Press, 1934.

———. *Psychoanalysis for Normal People*. Oxford University Press, 1932.

FREUD, SIGMUND. *General Introduction to Psychoanalysis*. New York, 1935.

GRODDECK, GEORG. *The World of Man*. London, 1935.

HADFIELD, J. A. *Psychology and Morals*. London, 1936.

HEYER, G. R. *The Organism of the Mind*. London, 1933.

HINKLE, BEATRICE. *The Recreating of the Individual*. New York, 1923.

HOWE, E. GRAHAM. *I and Me*. London, 1935.

———. *War Dance*. London, 1937.

———. *The Open Way*. London, 1939. (In collaboration with L. le Mesurier.)

JUNG, C. G. *Modern Man in Search of a Soul*. New York, 1933.

———. *Psychological Types*. New York, 1933.

———. *Psychology and Religion*. New Haven, 1938.

———. *Two Essays on Analytical Psychology*. New York, 1928.

———. *The Integration of Personality*. New York, 1939.

———. *The Secret of the Golden Flower*. New York, 1931. (With Richard Wilhelm.)

WHEELER, R. H. *The Laws of Human Nature*. New York, 1932.

WICKES, F. G. *The Inner World of Man*. New York, 1938.

WITTELS, FRITZ. *Freud and His Time*. New York, 1931.

THE MEANING OF HAPPINESS

ORIENTAL PSYCHOLOGY AND RELIGION

BALLOU, ROBERT. *The Bible of the World.* New York, 1939.

BECK, L. ADAMS. *The Story of Oriental Philosophy.* New York, 1931.

BESANT, ANNIE. *The Bhagavad-Gita.* London, 1918. (With Bhagavan Das.)

BUDDHIST LODGE. *What Is Buddhism?* London, 1931.

————. *Concentration and Meditation.* London, 1935.

CARUS, PAUL. *The Gospel of Buddha.* Chicago, 1894.

CH'U TA-KAO. *Tao Te Ching.* London, 1937.

CRANMER-BYNG, L. *The Vision of Asia.* London and New York, 1932.

DAVIDS, C. A. F. RHYS. *Manual of Buddhism.* London, 1932.

————. *Outlines of Buddhism.* London, 1934.

————. *What Was the Original Gospel in Buddhism?* London, 1938.

DEUSSEN, PAUL. *Outline of the Vedanta.* New York, 1907.

DVIVEDI, M. N. *The Yoga-Sutras of Patanjali.* Madras, 1934.

GILES, H. A. *Chuang Tzu.* Shanghai and London, 1926.

GILES, LIONEL. *Musings of a Chinese Mystic* (Chuang Tzu). London and New York, 1920.

————. *Taoist Teachings* (Lieh Tzu). London and New York, 1925.

GODDARD, DWIGHT. *A Buddhist Bible.* Thetford, Vt., 1938.

GUENON, RENÉ. *Man and His Becoming.* London, 1928.

LEGGE, JAMES. *Yi King.* Oxford University Press, 1882.

MASCARO, JUAN. *Himalayas of the Soul.* London and New York, 1938.

OKAKURA, K. *The Book of Tea.* Edinburgh, 1919.

OTTO, RUDOLF. *Mysticism of East and West.* London, 1932.

PRATT, J. B. *The Pilgrimage of Buddhism.* New York, 1928.

RADHAKRISHNAN, S. *Vedanta.* London, 1928.

————. *Philosophy of the Upanishads.* London, 1935.

SENZAKI, NYOGEN. *The Gateless Gate.* Los Angeles, 1934.

SUZUKI, B. L. *Mahayana Buddhism.* London, 1938.

SUZUKI, D. T. *Essays in Zen Buddhism.* 3 vols. London and Kyoto, 1927, 1933, 1934.

————. *Introduction to Zen Buddhism.* Kyoto, 1934.

————. *Die Grosse Befreiung.* With an Introduction by C. G. Jung. Leipzig, 1939. (German translation of the above.)

BIBLIOGRAPHY

SUZUKI, D. T. *Manual of Zen Buddhism.* Kyoto, 1935.

——. *Lankavatara Sutra.* London, 1932.

——. *Studies in the Lankavatara Sutra.* London, 1930.

VIVEKANANDA, SWAMI. *Raja Yoga, Karma Yoga, Jnana Yoga, Bhakti Yoga.* All in various eds. by the Advaita Ashrama, Almora, India.

WALEY, ARTHUR. *The Way and Its Power* (Tao Te Ching). London, 1935.

WATTS, ALAN W. *The Spirit of Zen.* London and New York, 1936.

——. *The Legacy of Asia and Western Man.* London, 1937; Chicago, 1938.

WONG MOW LAM. *Sutra of the Sixth Patriarch.* Shanghai, 1930.

WOODROFFE, JOHN. *Shakti and Shakta.* London and Madras, 1929.

MISCELLANEOUS

BERDYAEV, NICOLAS. *Freedom and the Spirit.* London, 1935.

ECKHART, MEISTER. *Meister Eckhart's Sermons.* Trans. Claud Field. Allenson, London, n.d.

JAMES, M. R. *The Apocryphal New Testament.* Oxford University Press, 1924.

JAMES, WILLIAM. *Varieties of Religious Experience.* New York and London, 1929.

KEYSERLING, HERMANN. *Creative Understanding.* London and New York, 1929.

MEAD, G. R. S. *Fragments of a Faith Forgotten.* London, 1931.

STARBUCK, E. D. *Psychology of Religion.* London, 1899.

UNDERHILL, EVELYN. *Mysticism.* London, 1930.

INDEX

INDEX

216

INDEX

217

INDEX

Material vs. spiritual, 42, 43
Maya, 24, 72, 142 ff., 178, 203 n.
Meditation, 146
Meher Baba, 26
Men, American, early deaths of, 27
    emotional attitude, 113 et seq.
Metaphysics, 81, 139
Methodism, 19
Mitrinovic, Dmitrije, 198
Monasticism, Buddhist, 148, 157
Monoimus, 188
Moods, 85, 104
Morality, 34, 50-51, 58, 127, 131,
    136, 195, 197 ff.
    Buddhist, 157
    Puritan, 19
    Three stages of, 67
Mother, the Terrible, 87
Mumon, 171
Mu-mon-kwan, 169
Mundaka Upanishad, 141
Music, analogy of, 40-41, 53, 190
Mystic, the, 41-42, 183
Mysticism, 23, 199
    Christian, 69

Nature, man's relation to, 10 et seq.
Nazism, 79
"Neti, neti . . . ," 145
Neurosis, 85, 88, 89 ff.
New Testament, 62
Nilambara-Vajrapani, 77
Nirvana, 151 ff., 153, 155 ff., 163,
    165, 197
Non-dualism, 64, 130, 142 ff., 164
    ff.
Novalis, 95

Obsession, 75, 82
Occultism, 42 ff., 140
Œdipus complex, 85
Old age, 53
Old Testament, 19
Omar Khayyam, 174
Opposites, pairs of, 2, 3 ff., 193 ff.
Ouspensky, P. D., 26
Oxherding Pictures, the Ten, 98

Pacifism, 63
Pain, 54, 125
Pali Canon, 148 et seq., 152
Pantheism, 141, 142
Participation mystique, 66, 82
Pastoral Psychologists, 90, 205 n.
Patanjali, 30
Personality, 192 et seq.
Phobias, 76, 85
Play, 123
Pleasure, 33-34, 37 ff., 52 ff.
Possession, psychic, 84, 112
Pralaya, 144
Predestination, 182
Pride, spiritual, 132, 133, 156, 180
Primitive, the, 79
Prinzhorn, H., 90
Prodigal Son, parable of, 12 ff., 66,
    120
Progress, ideal of, 20, 21
Protestantism, 18, 136
Psychic powers, 48
    vs. spiritual, 42, 43
Psychosis, 85
Ptah, 24
Puritanism, 18, 59
Pythagoreans, 134

Rationalism, 20-21
Rationalization, 22
Reason, 18, 20, 75 ff., 116
Reincarnation, 54
Relaxation, xx
Renaissance, 17
Repression, 60
Resurrection of the body, 34
Rinzai, 167, 168, 209 n.
Ritual, 196
Romans, Epistle to, 62
Rosicrucianism, 26

St. Athanasius, 182
St. Augustine, 120, 130, 195
St. Catherine of Genoa, 142
St. Francis of Assisi, 122
St. Michael and the Dragon, 57, 63
    ff., 68, 127
St. Paul, 62, 131, 136, 158

INDEX